Train-the-Trainer

Third Edition

Participant Coursebook

Penny L. Ittner
Alex F. Douds

HRD Press
22 Amherst Road
Amherst, Massachusetts 01002

Copyright © 2004, Human Technology, Inc.

Published by: Human Resource Development Press, Inc.
22 Amherst Road
Amherst, Massachusetts 01002
413-253-3488
800-822-2801 (U.S. and Canada)
413-253-3490 (fax)
www.hrdpress.com

All rights reserved. No part of this publication may be reproduced or transmitted in any form or by any means, electronic or mechanical, including photocopy, recording, or by information storage and retrieval system, without written permission from the publisher.

ISBN 0-87425-751-4

Editorial Services by Suzanne Bay
Production Services by Jean Miller
Cover Design by Eileen Klockars

Contents

About the Authors v

Lesson 1: Introduction and Overview 1-1

Lesson 2: Using Adult Learning Principles 2-1

Lesson 3: Analyzing the Training Requirements 3-1

Lesson 4: Developing Learning Objectives 4-1

Lesson 5: Outlining the Training Content 5-1

Lesson 6: Selecting Training Methods 6-1

Lesson 7: Developing and Using Training Aids 7-1

Lesson 8: Developing a Lesson Plan 8-1

Lesson 9: Using Basic Facilitation Skills 9-1

Lesson 10: Handling Problem Situations 10-1

Lesson 11: Practice Training 11-1

Lesson 12: Evaluating Training 12-1

Lesson 13: Using the Training Skills 13-1

Appendix: Job Aids

About the Authors

Penny Ittner has worked in the human resources field for the past 25 years, seven as training manager at a Fortune 100 company, where she was responsible for meeting the professional development needs of the 500-member training staff. For the past 19 years, she has been an independent consultant, helping people gain the skills they need to operate effectively in industry or government. Trainer training has been one of her primary areas of focus.

Penny has trained over 1,000 individuals who are responsible for employee training in their own organizations. Her private-sector client organizations include Microsoft, Air Products and Chemicals, Verizon, Johnson Laboratories, the Artery Organization, and General Dynamics. Her public-sector clients include the U.S. Department of Agriculture, U.S. Department of Health and Human Services, U.S. Department of Justice, U.S. Naval Reserves, and the Federal Judicial Center. Penny currently serves as adjunct associate professor at the University of Maryland University College, where she teaches undergraduate courses in the business and management program.

Alex Douds has over 20 years of broad experience in the training and development field. As director of the Performance Skills Group, a Division of Human Technology, Inc., he has led more than 125 performance improvement projects for private- and public-sector clients. His specialties include the design and implementation of "best practice" human resource management processes and learning systems, team performance systems, and workforce productivity programs. He also focuses on the design, development, and delivery of executive, management, and supervisory training programs, as well as on the development of multi-tiered, competency-based curricula.

Alex's private-sector client list includes such companies as General Dynamics, H.B. Fuller, Blue Cross and Blue Shield, Genzyme, AGFA, and the Ford Motor Company. Public-sector clients include the National Imagery and Mapping Agency, Defense Systems Information Agency, Federal Aviation Administration, U.S. Department of Justice, and the U.S. Department of Health and Human Services.

Lesson 1
Introduction and Overview

Contents

Overview	1-1
Workshop Overview	1-1
Workshop Objectives	1-2
Workshop Plan	1-2
Lesson Objectives	1-2
Definition of Training	1-3
Personal Resources and Learning Goals	1-3
Summary	1-4

Overview

In this lesson, you will be given an overview of the workshop, which will include the topics that will be covered and the basic workshop procedures that will be followed.

The lesson also includes general information about the training process. You will be introduced to the skills related to developing and conducting training that will be covered during the workshop.

Finally, you will have a chance to identify the training-related strengths you already possess, as well as your personal learning goals associated with this workshop.

Workshop Overview

The purpose of this workshop is to help you learn how to develop and conduct effective training. It is designed for "non-trainers"—people such as yourself who train on an occasional basis. It covers the basic skills necessary for you to effectively develop and conduct the training you are asked to do in your job.

You will see a variety of examples of how the training skills you are learning are applied. One example will be carried throughout the workshop as a way of illustrating the training activities that are covered. This example will be based on a hypothetical training situation that might occur in any organization.

Throughout this course, you will be an active participant in the learning process. It is a fact that people learn more in training when they are actively involved. "Learning by doing" is a basic principle followed in this workshop.

The workshop format includes group discussions and individual and group exercises designed to help you learn training skills. You will develop a practice training lesson and conduct a 15-minute segment of it during the workshop. Your fellow participants will be your "trainees" during your practice training.

Train-the-Trainer Participant Coursebook

Workshop Objectives

By the end of this workshop, you will be able to:

- Develop a training lesson geared to the learning needs of adults.
- Conduct training using the training lesson you developed.

Workshop Plan

Table 1-1 provides an overview of the lesson included in the workshop.

Table 1-1. Workshop Plan

Day	Lesson	Title
1	1 2 3 4	Introduction and Overview Using Adult Learning Principles Analyzing the Training Requirements Developing Learning Objectives
2	5 6 7 8	Outlining the Training Content Selecting Training Methods Developing and Using Training Aids Developing a Lesson Plan
3	9 10 11	Using basic Facilitation Skills Handling Problem Situations Practice Training (Preparation)
4	11 12 13	Practice Training (Delivery) Evaluating Training Using the Training Skills

Lesson Objectives

At the end of this lesson, you will be able to:

- Identify ways that training skills can be used at work.
- Describe the personal resources and learning goals you bring to the workshop.

Lesson 1: Introduction and Overview

Definition of Training

This workshop is focused on helping you learn training skills. We define **training** as the development and delivery of information that people will *use after attending the training.*

This definition distinguishes "training" from other situations where people are provided with information yet are *not necessarily* expected to *use the information they are given.* The distinction between training and non-training is an important one because the *process* for developing and delivering the information differs between the two.

Effective training requires that you have a clear picture of how the trainees will need to use the information after the training. It also requires that people *practice* what they have learned *before* they apply it. This practice step is not required in non-training situations, since the people are not necessarily going to use the information subsequent to the training. You will learn how to incorporate *practice* into the training you develop and conduct back at your job.

Personal Resources and Learning Goals

The worksheet shown in Table 1-2 provides a format for recording your personal resources and learning goals. This self-assessment will help you focus your efforts during this workshop. Feel free to add to your lists, as additional personal resources or goals become apparent to you during the workshop.

Train-the-Trainer Participant Coursebook

Table 1-2. Personal Resources and Learning Goals

RESOURCES I BRING	LEARNING GOALS

Summary

In this lesson, you introduced yourselves to one another. You were given an overview of the workshop and some general information about the training process. You also identified your own and others' personal resources and learning goals associated with this workshop.

In Lesson 2, you will learn about using adult learning principles in developing and conducting your training. These principles must be applied if your training is to be effective.

Lesson 2
Using Adult Learning Principles

Contents

Overview	2-1
Lesson Objectives	2-1
A Survey to Identify Learning Style	2-2
Differences between Children and Adults as Learners	2-5
Adult Learning Principles	2-6
Exercise: Applying Adult Learning Principles to Past Experiences	2-7
Summary	2-8

Overview

This lesson will cover learning styles and principles associated with adult learning. These are important elements to learn and use throughout the training process. If you do so, you increase the likelihood that your adult learners will learn.

Lesson Objectives

By the end of this lesson, you will be able to:

- Identify your own learning styles and those of others.
- Describe key principles to follow in helping adults learn.

Train-the-Trainer Participant Coursebook

A Survey to Identify Learning Style

Directions: Use this survey to determine your dominant learning style. For each statement appearing in the right column below, circle a code in the left column. Use the following scale:

SA = Strongly Agree
A = Agree
D = Disagree
SD = Strongly Disagree

If you neither agree nor disagree with a statement, then mark the code that most closely approximates your feelings about it.

Your Responses	Statements
SA A D SD	1. I learn best by listening to others.
SA A D SD	2. Whenever I need information, I usually look it up in a book or manual.
SA A D SD	3. Whenever I encounter a problem on the job, I usually ask a co-worker what to do to solve it.
SA A D SD	4. I like to read in my spare time.
SA A D SD	5. Of all the courses I completed in school, I enjoyed English the most.
SA A D SD	6. I learn best by watching others.
SA A D SD	7. Whenever I am learning something new, I usually find it necessary to watch other people before I can apply the skill properly myself.
SA A D SD	8. I like to watch television or movies in my spare time.
SA A D SD	9. Other people have sometimes kidded me because I tend to imitate behaviors of people I admire.
SA A D SD	10. Of all the courses I completed in school, I tended to like those in which I had an opportunity to imitate the behaviors of other people.

(Continued on next page . . .)

Source: *The Structured On-the-Job Training Workshop* by Dr. William J. Rothwell. Copyright © 1990 by Human Resource Development Press, Inc.

Lesson 2: Using Adult Learning Principles

A Survey to Identify Learning Style (continued)

Your Responses				Statements
SA	A	D	SD	11. I learn best by doing things.
SA	A	D	SD	12. Whenever I am learning something new, I usually find it necessary to try out the new knowledge or skill before I can be effective in using it.
SA	A	D	SD	13. During my spare time, I enjoy participating in sports.
SA	A	D	SD	14. Other people have pointed out that I like to "jump in and get my feet wet" on new projects or tasks.
SA	A	D	SD	15. Of all the courses I had in school, I preferred those that I thought were "practical"—that is, courses that taught me things that I could use right away.
SA	A	D	SD	16. I learn best by first trying something out and then having someone else let me know what I did "right" and "wrong."
SA	A	D	SD	17. When I am learning something new, I usually find it necessary to "jump in there and do it," and then have someone else help me figure out what I did well and not so well.
SA	A	D	SD	18. I enjoy activities that require me to *do something* and then measure my own progress.
SA	A	D	SD	19. Other people frequently give me advice, and I like that.
SA	A	D	SD	20. Of all the courses I completed while in school, I preferred those in which the teacher gave me general goals to achieve and then prompt, specific feedback on how well I achieved the goals.

(Continued on next page)

A Survey to Identify Learning Style (continued)

Directions: Examine each code you marked on the survey and assign it the following points:

Strongly Agree = 4 points
Agree = 3 points
Disagree = 2 points
Strongly Disagree = 1 point

- Total your scores on items 1–5 and place the answer in the box below those items on the survey.

- Total your scores on items 6–10 and place the answer in the box below those items on the survey.

- Total your scores on items 11–15 and place the answer in the box below those items on the total survey.

- Total your scores on items 16–20 and place the answer in the box below those items on the survey.

THEN... Place the four scores in the boxes below:

Scores for ITEMS 1–5	Scores for ITEMS 6–10	Scores for ITEMS 11–15	Scores for ITEMS 16–20

- If your score on items 1–5 exceeds all other scores, then your Learning Style is dominated by **listening and reading.**

- If your score on items 6–10 exceeds all other scores, then your Learning Style is dominated by **observing and imitating.**

- If your score on items 11–15 exceeds all other scores, then your Learning Style is dominated by **doing.**

- If your score on items 16–20 exceeds all other scores, then your Learning Style is dominated by **receiving feedback.**

- If your scores on two groups of items are tied, then you have more than one major learning style.

Lesson 2: Using Adult Learning Principles

Differences between Children and Adults as Learners

Often when people are asked to assume a trainer role, they begin with an image of training based on how they have been taught in the past. In most instances, the image in their minds is closely related to how they were taught as children in school. But there are significant differences between children and adults *as learners*. The training approach to be used with adults, therefore, is significantly different from the approach that would be appropriate for teaching children. It is important to understand the differences, so that you can gear your training to the needs of your adult learners.

Table 2-1 below lists some primary differences between children and adults as learners.

Table 2-1. Differences between Children and Adults as Learners

CHILDREN	ADULTS
Rely on others to decide what is important to be learned.	Decide for themselves what is important to be learned.
Accept the information being presented at face value.	Need to verify the information, based on their beliefs and experiences.
Expect what they are learning to be useful in their long-term future.	Expect what they are learning to be immediately useful.
Have little or no experience upon which to draw—are relatively "clean slates."	Have much past experience upon which to draw—might have fixed viewpoints.
Have little ability to serve as a knowledgeable resource to teacher or fellow classmates.	Have significant ability to serve as a knowledgeable resource to the trainer and fellow learners.

Adult Learning Principles

The differences between children and adults as learners point out the need to follow specific principles when training adults. Table 2-2 below lists eight principles you can use to help adults learn.

Table 2-2. Adult Learning Principles

1. Focus on **real world** problems.
2. Emphasize how the learning can be applied.
3. Relate the learning to the goals of the learner.
4. Relate the materials to the past experiences of the learner.
5. Allow debate and challenge of ideas.
6. Listen to and respect the opinions of learners.
7. Encourage learners to be resources to you and to one another.
8. Treat learners like adults.

Lesson 2: Using Adult Learning Principles

Exercise: Applying Adult Learning Principles To Past Experiences

The purpose of this exercise is to help you verify the adult learning principles by applying them to your own past experiences as an adult learner. Follow the instructions outlined below. When you have finished, you will be asked to discuss your conclusions with another person in the group.

1. Think of one training session you attended in the past that was **ineffective** for you as an adult learner. Jot down the ineffective elements in the appropriate space on the worksheet below. Then try to associate the ineffective elements with the adult learning principles shown in Table 2-2 on page 2-6. Enter in the appropriate space on the worksheet which principles you think were being **ignored** (by number).

INEFFECTIVE ELEMENTS	PRINCIPLES IGNORED

2. Now think of one training session you attended in the past that was **effective** for you, as an adult learner. Jot down the effective elements in the appropriate space below. Then try to associate the effective elements with the adult learning principles in Figure 2-2. Enter in the appropriate space on the worksheet which principles were being **followed** (use the numbers on the chart).

EFFECTIVE ELEMENTS	PRINCIPLES FOLLOWED

Train-the-Trainer Participant Coursebook

Summary

In this lesson, you learned about your own learning styles and those of others. You were also provided with adult learning principles that you can use in your training. By taking into account learning styles and adult learning principles while you develop and conduct training, you increase the likelihood that learning will occur.

This workshop is based on the four learning styles and the eight adult learning principles you learned in this lesson. As the workshop continues, notice how these concepts are being applied.

In the next lesson, we will cover the first activity in developing training—analyzing the training requirement.

Lesson 3
Analyzing the Training Requirement

Contents

Overview	3-1
Lesson Objective	3-1
Analyzing the Training Requirement	3-2
Elements to Consider	3-3
Worksheet for Analyzing the Training Requirement	3-4
Example: Analyzing the Training Requirement	3-6
Exercise: Analyzing the Training Requirement	3-9
Summary	3-12

Overview

In the first lesson of this workshop, you were introduced to the skills involved in developing and conducting training that will be covered in this workshop.

This lesson covers the first skill—analyzing the training requirement. You will learn the important elements to consider in analyzing the training requirement (need), and you will be provided with a worksheet that will help you in performing your analysis. During the lesson, you will have an opportunity to practice using the worksheet, as you analyze the training requirement associated with the material you brought with you to the workshop.

Lesson Objective

By the end of this lesson, you will be able to:

- Analyze a training need or requirement.

Analyzing the Training Requirement

Introduction

As someone who trains on an occasional basis, you are likely to become aware of a training need in one of two ways:

1. **You personally identify the need.**
   For example, you might notice that employees are having difficulty implementing a policy change, or you may be aware that new employees need training on a particular job task.

2. **Others identify the need.**
   Perhaps you are asked to train people who need to learn about your area of specialty, or you are temporarily assigned to develop training on a project to be implemented in your organization.

Whether the need for training is self-determined or determined by others, your first step is to **analyze the training need or requirement.**

Purpose

The purpose of analyzing the training need or requirement is to help you plan for the major elements that will be involved in your training. You should begin the analysis as soon as possible after you are aware of the training requirement, even if you **know** you do not have all the information you will need. Early analysis will help you identify the areas requiring your attention, **including** areas where you will have to gather more information in order to appropriately plan for the training.

Lesson 3: Analyzing the Training Requirement

Elements to Consider

There are six elements to consider when analyzing the training need. Table 3-1 shows the six elements and gives a brief description of each one.

Table 3-1. Elements to Consider in Analyzing a Training Need or Requirement

ELEMENT	DESCRIPTION
1. Statement of training need	The requestor's statement of the training need.
2. Why is training required?	Identification of the requestor, the consequences of providing/not providing training, and the desired effects on learner job performance.
3. Who are the participants?	Identification of the participants, their familiarity with the training content, and anticipated participant reactions to the training.
4. What's the training content?	The nature of the training content, possible resources, and anticipated difficulties in developing the content.
5. What are the timing issues?	The starting date, length/frequency of the training, and any known timing issues.
6. Where will the training be conducted?	The location and number of participants, and an assessment of the space, equipment, and other resources that are needed and available.

Worksheet for Analyzing the Training Requirement

Table 3-2 on the next page provides a worksheet for analyzing a training requirement. It also includes guidelines for you to follow in recording the information for each item on the worksheet.

Train-the-Trainer Participant Coursebook

Table 3-2. Worksheet for Analyzing the Training Requirement
(page 1 of 2)

Today's date: _____

1. **Statement of training need requested**
   Record the training need, as stated by the requestor. If *you* have identified the need, write a statement of the need as you view it.

2. **Why is training required?**
   a. Source of request:

   b. Expected benefits:

   c. Negative consequences if training is not delivered:

   d. New/changed behavior desired:

3. **Who are the participants?**
   a. Categories/size of participant group:

   b. Familiarity with training content:

4. **What's the training content?**
   a. Content:
      Identify the general nature of the training content, such as the subject, topics, or job task involved.

   b. Available supportive resources:
      Note the resources for use in developing the training (documentation, subject-matter experts, training programs).

Lesson 3: Analyzing the Training Requirement

**Table 3-2. Worksheet for Analyzing the Training Requirement
(page 1 of 2)**

4. **What's the training content?** (continued)

   c. **Issues/problems in formulating content:**
   Record any difficulties you might have in determining the training content.

   d. **Anticipated reactions/problems with content/training:**
   Record an assessment of anticipated participant attitudes about the training. Identify any potential problems participants have regarding the training content or other aspects of the training.

5. **What are the timing issues?**

   a. **Start/complete dates:**
   Record the actual or approximate date(s) the training is to begin and end.

   b. **Length of Training:**
   Record the specific or estimated number of training hours or days.

   c. **Frequency of Training:**
   Record how many training sessions will occur and how often.

   d. **Time Issues:**
   Identify any issues related to the time details of the training.

6. **Where will the training be conducted?**

   a. **Physical location:**
   Record the location(s) where the training will take place.

   b. **Estimated number of participants:**
   Record the estimated number of participants to be trained at one time.

   c. **Adequacy of space and delivery resources needed:**
   Assess the size, accessibility of space, and the adequacy of equipment and other resources that are needed and available.

Example:
Analyzing the Training Requirement

Orientation to the Hypothetical Training Situation

A primary concern of organizations today is that their employees carry out job responsibilities in accordance with certain ethical standards. "Ethics training" is one way organizations have of making sure that these standards are understood and complied with.

In the hypothetical situation you are about to encounter, Chris, an employee of one of the organization's line operations, has been loaned to the Human Resources Department to develop and conduct ethics training for employees currently on the payroll. To help prepare her for this responsibility, Chris has recently completed a **Train-the-Trainer** workshop. This will be her first opportunity to apply the training skills she learned in that workshop.

Where does Chris begin?

Chris remembers that the first thing to do is to *analyze the training requirement.* Table 3-3 shows the *Analyzing the Training Requirement* worksheet that Chris prepared.

Lesson 3: Analyzing the Training Requirement

**Table 3-3. Example of Completed Worksheet for
Analyzing the Training Requirement**

Today's date: _____

1. **Statement of training need requested**

   Ethics training is needed for all employees in the organization.

2. **Why is training required?**

   a. **Source of request:**

   HR vice president

   b. **Expected benefits:**

   Employees will operate in accordance with prescribed ethical standards.

   c. **Negative consequences if training is not delivered:**

   Confusion, inconsistent behaviors, potential lawsuits.

   d. **New/changed behavior desired:**

   When confronted with "difficult" or potentially ambiguous situations, employees will follow the appropriate guidelines for ethical behavior.

3. **Who are the participants?**

   a. **Categories/size of participant group:**

   Supervisory employees—10
   Customer service employees—150
   Support employees—15

   b. **Familiarity with the training content:**

   Supervisory employees have the most familiarity with the content. Other employees who have been in the organization for some time will be more familiar with it than newer employees. All might have misperceptions, though.

4. **What's the training content?**

   a. **Content:**

   General rules, standards of ethical behavior
   Specific situations and ethical responses to them

**Table 3-3. Example of Completed Worksheet for
Analyzing the Training Requirement (continued)**

4. **What's the training content?** (continued)

   b. **Available supportive resources (documentation, subject-matter experts, other training packages, etc.):**

   Documented guidelines
   Help from legal staff

   c. **Issues/problems in formulating content:**

   None known at this time.

   d. **Anticipated reactions/problems with content/training:**

   Some employees might view the training as wasted time because they are overloaded with work. Newer employees will welcome clarifications to potentially difficult situations.

5. **What are the timing issues?**

   a. **Start/complete dates:**

   Begin approximately 7/1, and complete by 9/30.

   b. **Length of training:**

   1 day (maximum)

   c. **Frequency of training:**

   VP wants this training to be given to all new employees, with a shorter version ("refresher") to be given to all other employees once a year.

   d. **Time issues:**

   None known at this time.

6. **Where will the training be conducted?**

   a. **Physical location:**

   Not known at this time.

   b. **Estimated number of participants:**

   12 classes, 15 participants per class.

   c. **Adequacy of space and delivery resources needed:**

   Unknown. Might need delivery help.

Lesson 3: Analyzing the Training Requirement

Exercise:
Analyzing the Training Requirement

The purpose of this exercise is to give you practice in analyzing a training requirement.

Using the training ideas you have brought with you to the workshop, complete the "Analyzing the Training Requirement" worksheet on the following pages, based on that information. Consider the worksheet elements based on the need to develop and conduct the training in your work environment. If you do not have all the information you need at this time, fill out as much of the worksheet as you can. Refer to Tables 3-1, 3-2, and 3-3 as you complete your worksheet.

When you have finished, there will be a group discussion of this exercise, and volunteers will be asked to share their answers with the group.

Exercise:
Analyzing the Training Requirement

Today's date: _____

1. **Statement of training need requested**

2. **Why is training required?**
   a. Source of request:

   b. Expected benefits:

   c. Negative consequences if training is not delivered:

   d. New/changed behavior desired:

3. **Who are the participants?**
   a. Categories/size of participant group:

   b. Familiarity with training content:

4. **What's the training content?**
   a. Content:

   b. Available supportive resources:

Lesson 3: Analyzing the Training Requirement

Exercise: Analyzing the Training Requirement (continued)

4. **What's the training content?** (continued)

   c. **Issues/problems in formulating content:**

   d. **Anticipated reactions/problems with content/training:**

5. **What are the timing issues?**

   a. **Start/complete dates:**

   b. **Length of training:**

   c. **Frequency of training:**

   d. **Time issues:**

6. **Where will the training be conducted?**

   a. **Physical location:**

   b. **Estimated number of participants:**

   c. **Adequacy of space and delivery resources needed:**

Summary

In this lesson, you learned how to analyze a training requirement. You were introduced to a worksheet that can help you analyze a training requirement, and you practiced using the worksheet on the material you brought with you to the workshop. You will use the information you developed on your worksheet in subsequent lessons, as you continue learning the skills needed to develop and conduct training.

In Lesson 4 you will learn another skill—how to develop learning objectives for your training.

Lesson 4
Developing Learning Objectives

Contents

Overview	4-1
Lesson Objective	4-1
Learning Objectives	4-2
Steps in Developing Learning Objectives	4-3
Example: Developing Learning Objectives	4-5
Exercise 1: Assessing Learning Objectives	4-7
Exercise 2: Writing Learning Objectives	4-8
Summary	4-9

Overview

This lesson covers how to develop learning objectives for your training. This skill is critical because all your activities must be designed to help achieve those objectives.

In this lesson, you will learn how to identify and develop appropriate learning objectives that specify what participants will be able to do as a result of your training. You will return to the workshop example to learn how Chris completed the learning objectives for her training. Then you will practice developing learning objectives, using the information you developed in your training requirements analysis.

Lesson Objective

By the end of this lesson, you will be able to:

- Develop learning objectives.

Learning Objectives

Purpose

Learning objectives are the foundation of effective training. As you recall from Lesson 2, adults expect their training to be useful to them. When you develop adequate learning objectives, you are taking the first step in making sure that your training meets the needs of your adult participants.

Learning objectives help the trainer and the participant focus on the achievement of specific results.

1. They help the **trainer** focus on developing and conducting training that provides the participants with the skills and knowledge they need.

2. They provide the **participants** with a clear understanding of what they will be able to do as a result of the training.

Levels of Objectives

Learning objectives are developed at two levels—at the course level and at the lesson level. Course objectives, which are developed first, state the broad behavior expected of participants at the end of the course. Lesson objectives are subsequently developed; they state specific behaviors required to achieve the course objectives.

Example 1

Course Objective

"At the end of this workshop, you will be able to develop a training plan geared to the learning needs of adults."

Lesson Objective

"At the end of this lesson, you will be able to select appropriate training methods."

The above example shows one of the broad course objectives for this workshop—to develop a training plan. The narrower lesson objective—to select training methods—is one key element involved in developing a training plan.

Throughout this lesson, we will be focusing on objectives at the lesson level. However, the steps you will learn in developing lesson objectives apply to developing course objectives as well.

Lesson 4: Developing Learning Objectives

Steps in Developing Learning Objectives

There are two steps you must follow when developing adequate learning objectives. They are:

1. Clarify the tasks to be performed after training.

2. Develop appropriately stated objectives based on those tasks.

Clarifying After-Training Tasks

To clarify after-training tasks, start with the information you developed when you analyzed the training requirement. Review your worksheet, paying particular attention to Item 2d, where you identified the new or changed behavior expected of the participants. Then list the major tasks the participants will be doing as a result of your training.

Developing Appropriately Stated Objectives

Once you have clarified the after-training tasks, write objectives that describe the task behavior you want the participants to demonstrate during training.

Example 2

After-Training Task:

The participants will be communicating with employees about a policy change.

Learning Objective:

"At the end of this lesson, participants will be able to list significant changes in their unit's operation that could result from the policy change."

It is important that the learning objectives for your training come as close as possible to the actual behavior the participant will be expected to perform back on the job. In Example 2, it is more realistic to have the participants list the changes in writing, because they normally provide written information of this nature to their staff.

When you are describing desired behavior, use words that describe **observable** behavior. This will come easily when you are writing learning objectives for PHYSICAL SKILLS, such as operating a computer or performing CPR techniques.

When the behavior relates to participant KNOWLEDGE or ATTITUDES, however, you might be tempted to use words like *"know," "understand,"* or *"appreciate."* These words describe something that is happening *inside* a participant's head. In these cases, you must write learning objectives that use words that describe the **observable** behavior that the participants will demonstrate during training.

Example 3

After-Training Task:

The participants will make sure that all budget requests are signed by the appropriate party.

Learning Objective:

"At the end of the training, participants will be able to…

INCORRECT	CORRECT
know the importance of obtaining the appropriate signatures on budget requests."	***select budget requests*** on which the appropriate signatures have been obtained."

Example 4

After-Training Task:

The participants will be trying to convince community groups of the need for policy changes.

Learning Objective:

"At the end of the training, participants will be able to…

INCORRECT	CORRECT
appreciate how the policy changes will help the community."	***describe*** the positive impact the policy changes will have on the community."

In examples 2, 3, and 4 above, the correct learning objective included a word that described observable behavior that could be demonstrated in training. Table 4-1 offers examples of appropriate and inappropriate words used in writing learning objectives, based on whether or not they describe observable behavior.

Lesson 4: Developing Learning Objectives

Table 4-1. Example of Appropriate and Inappropriate Words for Writing Learning Objectives

APPROPRIATE WORDS (Observable Behavior)		INAPPROPRIATE WORDS (Behavior Not Observable)	
write	explain	accept	appreciate
classify	list	be aware of	believe
calculate	select	remember	comprehend
prepare	apply	recall	know
operate	choose	be familiar with	understand
define	construct	consider	discern
describe	complete	grasp	ascertain
demonstrate	identify	value	learn

Note: This is just a sample list. Whatever word you choose, remember that it is critical to communicate clearly the behavior that must be **shown** by the participant, so that the participant and the trainer each know that learning has taken place.

Finally, learning objectives should be expressed from the **participant's** point of view. You are defining what you want the **participant** to be able to do as a result of the training, **not** what you as the **trainer** want to accomplish. Starting all of your objectives with the phrase, "By the end of the training, the participants will be able to…" will help you to keep this in mind.

Example: Developing Learning Objectives

Let's continue our example of the request for ethics training to illustrate how learning objectives are developed.

As you remember, Chris's first step in responding to the need for training was to analyze the training requirement. Next, Chris will develop the learning objectives for the training.

Chris starts by referring back to the "Analyzing the Training Requirement" worksheet. Chris reviews all the information on the worksheet, paying particular attention to the new or changed behavior expected of the participants (Item 2d).

Note: Take a moment to review Table 3-3 in your Coursebook so you can follow along with Chris.

Chris knows the specific after-training tasks expected of the three training populations because Chris is an experienced supervisor responsible for customer service as well as support operations. Chris lists the major tasks the participants will be expected to do as a result of the training. These tasks will become the basis for learning objectives. (See Figure 4-2 on the following page.)

**Table 4-2. Example of After-Training
Tasks and Learning Objectives**

After-Training Tasks:	• Operate ethically in dealing with customers, suppliers, and other employees. • Report instances of actual or potential violation of ethical standards.
Learning Objectives:	• State the ethical standards required by the organization. • Identify appropriate behavior in circumstances involving ethical issues. • State correct procedures for reporting instances of ethical violations.

Lesson 4: Developing Learning Objectives

Exercise 1: Assessing Learning Objectives

The purpose of this exercise is to give you an opportunity to practice evaluating learning objectives and correcting those that are inadequate.

Read the learning objectives written below. Place checkmarks in the blanks beside objectives you think describe observable behavior. If you do not think an objective describes observable behavior, use the space below the objective to rewrite it. Refer to Table 4-1 for help as needed to complete the exercise.

When you have finished, there will be a group discussion of this exercise, and volunteers will be asked to share their answers with the group.

Note: Assume that the objectives appropriately reflect the after-training tasks to be performed by the trainees.

At the end of the training, participants will be able to:

_____ 1. State the purpose of the technology transfer function in their organization.

_____ 2. Know how to operate the office computer system.

_____ 3. Know which provisions of the new personnel policy require changes in hiring procedures.

_____ 4. Prepare a report on the results of the operational review.

_____ 5. Appreciate the importance of following the procedures outlined in the new manual.

4-7

Train-the-Trainer Participant Coursebook

Exercise 2: Writing Learning Objectives

The purpose of this exercise is to give you a chance to write a learning objective for the material you brought to the workshop.

Turn to Coursebook page 3-10 and take out the *Analyzing the Training Requirement* worksheet you completed.

Using the information you developed on your worksheet as a starting point, clarify the after-training tasks your participants should perform as a result of your training. Use the space below for recording those tasks.

_____
_____
_____
_____
_____
_____
_____
_____

Now use the space below to write **one** learning objective for your training, based on one of the above tasks. Remember to use an action word to describe the observable behavior you want participants to demonstrate in the training.

_____
_____
_____
_____
_____
_____
_____

When you have finished the exercise, there will be a group discussion, and volunteers will be asked to share their objectives with the group.

Lesson 4: Developing Learning Objectives

Summary

In this lesson, you learned how to develop learning objectives for your training program.

In Lesson 5, you will learn the next step in the training development process—outlining the training content.

Lesson 5
Outlining the Training Content

Contents

Overview	5-1
Lesson Objective	5-1
Outlining the Training Content	5-2
Steps in Outlining the Training Content	5-2
Example: Outlining the Training Content	5-4
Exercise: Outlining the Training Content	5-7
Summary	5-8

Overview

This lesson explains how to outline the training content for a learning objective. You will learn how to identify the action steps participants must perform and the knowledge required of them to perform those steps in order to meet the learning objective. These action steps and knowledge requirements form the basis of the training content for your lesson.

During the lesson, you will return to the workshop example to learn how Chris outlines the training content for the learning objectives for the ethics training. Then you will have a chance to outline the training content for the learning objective you developed earlier in the workshop.

Lesson Objective

By the end of this lesson, you will be able to:

- Outline the training content for a learning objective.

Outlining the Training Content

Definition and Purpose

The training content for a learning objective is everything the participant will have to do and know in order to achieve the learning objective. When you are developing the training content, you first identify the actions the participant must take to reach the learning objective, and then identify the knowledge the participant must have to complete those actions.

Outlining the training content serves three purposes:

1. It enables you to sort through the **possible** training content in order to identify the content that is really **necessary** for the participants to learn.

2. It allows you to organize and put in sequence the training content for presentation during the lesson.

3. It serves as a checking mechanism, so you can make sure that your training includes everything that participants will need to know and do to achieve the learning objective.

Outlining content is probably not a new concept for you. If you have ever had to write a paper or give a talk, you probably started by outlining the information. You will use the same type of skill in outlining the training content, but with one difference. You will be viewing the training content from the participant's perspective (what the participant needs in order to achieve the objective), rather than from your own perspective (what you as the trainer want to tell the participant).

Steps in Outlining the Training Content

There are two steps involved in outlining the training content. They are:

1. List the actions participants must take to accomplish the learning objective, as well as the knowledge required so participants can take those actions.

2. Put the training content (knowledge requirements and actions) into sequence, according to the order in which they will be covered.

Lesson 5: Outlining the Training Content

Step 1: Listing Actions and Knowledge Requirements (KRs)

Learning is most effective when the training content is broken down into small parts. The smaller the parts, the more easily they can be learned. Breaking the training content down into small parts will also help you make sure that nothing is left out.

As you begin to develop your list of actions, it sometimes helps to visualize someone performing the training tasks, even those involving mental actions. Imagine that the last action the person takes is the one stated in the learning objective. ("At the end of this lesson, participants will be able to: [action].")

An outline should include what the participants must do (actions), as well as the information that the participants must know and be able to manipulate correctly in order to take action (knowledge requirements, or KRs).

As you list each action, consider which information will be required to perform it. What **facts** or **rules** would a person need to know in order to perform? These are your **knowledge requirements.**

If you are unsure of the actions or knowledge requirements, clarify them now. Refer to the "available supportive resources" you identified earlier when you completed your worksheet for analyzing the training requirement.

Don't worry about oversimplifying the actions or knowledge requirements. Right now, you are only outlining the training content—not planning to conduct training. If you decide later on that they are too simplistic, you can easily combine them when you develop your training plan.

Example 1

Learning Objective:

> By the end of the lesson, participants will be able to describe significant changes in their unit's operation that might result from the policy change.

ACTION	KRs
Compare the new policy to the old.	Know the content included in both the new and old policy.
Identify significant changes.	Know criteria for classifying changes as significant.
Describe significant changes.	1. Know the variety of media available for describing changes. 2. Know how to employ available media appropriately.

Step 2: Sequencing Training Content

After you have identified all of the actions and knowledge requirements needed to achieve the objective, you are ready to put them in the order in which they should be presented.

As you go about performing a task, you **think** about certain information before **doing** something. As you start organizing your training content, remember the rule that knowledge requirements precede the actions to which they relate.

Example 2

Sequenced Training Content:

1. *Know the content included in the old policy as well as the new policy.*
2. *Compare the new policy to the old one.*
3. *Know criteria for classifying changes as significant.*
4. *Identify significant changes.*
5. *Know the variety of media available for describing changes.*
6. *Know how to employ available media appropriately.*
7. *Describe significant changes.*

Example: Outlining the Training Content

Let's look again at our example of ethics training to see how Chris goes about outlining the training content for the objectives.

So far, Chris has analyzed the training requirement and developed learning objectives. As you recall, there are three learning objectives for the training session. Chris must now outline the training content for each objective.

Chris lists the **actions** participants must take in accomplishing each learning objective and what participants would have to **know** in order to take those actions.

Finally, Chris organizes the training content according to when it should be presented in training, following the principle that knowledge requirements precede actions (the KRs).

Table 5-1 shows Chris's completed training content outline for the three objectives.

Lesson 5: Outlining the Training Content

Table 5-1. Example of Training Content Outline

Learning Objective: By the end of the lesson, participants will be able to state the ethical standards required by the organization.

    Action: *State the ethical standards required by the organization.*

    KRs: *Know the established ethical standards.*

Learning Objective: By the end of the lesson, participants will be able to identify appropriate behavior in circumstances involving ethical issues.

    Action: *Identify circumstances involving ethical issues.*

    KRs: *Know the factors that define circumstances as those involving ethical issues.*

    Action: *Choose appropriate behavior in dealing with ethical circumstances.*

    KRs: *Know behaviors appropriate in ethical situations.*

Learning Objective: By the end of the lesson, participants will be able to state correct procedures for reporting instances of ethical violations.

    Action: *Identify reportable ethical violations.*

    KRs: *Know the definition of "reportable violation."*

    Action: *State the correct procedures for reporting ethical violations.*

    KRs: *Know the correct procedures.*

Sequenced Training Content:
1. *Established ethical standards required by the organization.*
2. *Factors that define circumstances as those involving ethical issues.*
3. *Examples of past ethical violations.*
4. *Behaviors appropriate in dealing with ethical situations.*
5. *Definition of reportable ethical violations.*
6. *Correct procedures for reporting ethical violations.*

Exercise: Outlining the Training Content

The purpose of this exercise is to give you the opportunity to outline the training content for the learning objective you developed earlier in the workshop.

Follow the instructions shown below to complete the exercise. When you have finished, there will be a group discussion about the exercise.

Instructions:

1. Turn to the learning objective you developed during Lesson 4 (Coursebook page 4-8) and record the objective on the worksheet on the following page.

2. Next, list an **action** participants must take in accomplishing the learning objective. Record the **knowledge requirements (KRs)** associated with that action.

3. Continue to list the actions and knowledge requirements for your objective.

4. Finally, organize the training content according to how and when it should be presented in training, observing the principle that knowledge requirements precede actions. List the content, in sequence, on the worksheet.

Lesson 5: Outlining the Training Content

Exercise: Outlining the Training Content (concluded)

Learning Objective: By the end of the lesson, participants will be able to:

Actions and KRs:

Sequenced Training Content:

Train-the-Trainer Participant Coursebook

Summary

In this lesson, you learned how to develop an outline for a specific learning objective. You learned to identify all of the actions and knowledge necessary in order for participants to achieve the objective, and to organize the content based on how and when it should be presented in training. You will re-work the training content you outlined in this lesson when you develop your training plan later in this workshop.

In Lesson 6, you will learn about training methods. During that lesson, you will be thinking about the kinds of approaches you can use to cover the training content you just outlined.

Lesson 6
Selecting Training Methods

Contents

Overview	6-1
Lesson Objective	6-1
Selecting Training Methods	6-2
Criteria for Selection	6-4
Example: Selecting Training Methods	6-7
Exercise: Selecting Training Methods	6-9
Summary	6-10

Overview

This lesson covers six methods commonly used in training. You will learn about these six methods and criteria to use in selecting the best ones for your training.

During the lesson, you will see Chris do some early thinking about methods to use in her ethics training. You will also get a chance to do some preliminary selection of training methods based on the training content you outlined in Lesson 5.

Lesson Objective

By the end of this lesson, you will be able to:

- Select appropriate training methods.

Selecting Training Methods

Definition and Purpose

Once you have outlined the training content for a learning objective, as you did in Lesson 5, you will begin to think about approaches for teaching that content. These approaches are called **training methods.**

Training methods serve two important purposes:

1. They provide a means to learn the specific training content you have outlined.

2. They keep participants interested and involved in the training, thus enhancing their learning.

Types of Training Methods

There are many training methods available to you as a trainer. In this lesson, we will focus on six of the most commonly used methods. They are:

1. Case study
2. Demonstration
3. Group discussion
4. Role play
5. Structured exercise
6. Trainer presentation

Table 6-1 provides a brief description, and gives examples of each of these methods.

Lesson 6: Selecting Training Methods

Table 6-1. Training Methods

METHOD	DESCRIPTION
Case Study	Participants are given information about a situation and directed to come to decisions or solve a problem concerning the situation. Can be brief or lengthy. (You will see Chris use a case study later in the workshop.)
Demonstration	Participants are shown the correct steps for completing a task, or are shown an example of a correctly completed task. (The Coursebook segments describing the hypothetical ethics training have been used to show examples of correctly completed tasks.)
Group Discussion	The trainer leads the participants in discussing a particular topic. (Earlier in this lesson, your trainer led a group discussion about the particular workshop activities you and your fellow participants have enjoyed the most.)
Role Play	Participants "act out" a situation while others observe and analyze. (This training method will be used later in the workshop.)
Structured Exercise	Participants take part in an exercise that enables them to practice new skills. (The exercises you have completed throughout the workshop have been structured exercises.)
Trainer Presentation	The trainer presents new information orally to participants. (Your trainer made a brief presentation to introduce the six training methods taught in this lesson.)

Criteria for Selection

There are three general criteria that you must take into consideration when you are selecting methods for your training. These are shown in Table 6-2 below.

Table 6-2. General Selection Criteria

CRITERIA	EXPLANATION
1. The Learning Objective	Will the method most effectively lead the participant toward the accomplishment of the learning objective?
2. The Participants	Does the method take into account the size, experience levels, and other special characteristics of the group?
3. The Practical Requirements	Is the method feasible, given the physical environment, time (both preparation and classroom time), materials, and any cost limitations you have?

Keeping these three general criteria in mind, also consider the advantages and drawbacks of specific training methods. Table 6-3 lists some of the advantages and drawbacks in connection with the six methods covered in this lesson.

Lesson 6: Selecting Training Methods

Table 6-3. Advantages and Drawbacks of Training Methods
(page 1 of 2)

METHOD	ADVANTAGES	DRAWBACKS
Case Study	Requires active involvement. Can simulate performance required after training. Learning can be observed.	Information must be precise and kept up-to-date. Needs sufficient class time for participants to complete the case. Participants can become too interested in the case content.
Demonstration	Aids in understanding and retention. Stimulates participant interest. Can give participants a model to follow.	Must be accurate and relevant to participants. Written examples can require lengthy preparation time. Trainer demonstrations might not be clearly visible to all participants.
Group Discussion	Keeps participants interested and involved. Participant resources can be discovered and shared. Learning can be observed.	Learning points can be confusing or even lost. A few participants might dominate the discussion. Time control is more difficult.
Role Play	Requires active involvement. Can simulate performance required after training. Allows participants to "try out" new behavior.	Can be viewed as threatening or useless by participants. Participants might not play their roles accurately. Requires careful planning and administrative control.

Table 6-3. Advantages and Drawbacks of Training Methods
(page 2 of 2)

METHOD	ADVANTAGES	DRAWBACKS
Structured Exercise	Aids in retention. Allows practice of new skills in a controlled environment. Participants are actively involved.	Requires preparation time. Might be difficult to relate to all participant situations. Needs sufficient class time for exercise completion and feedback.
Trainer Presentation	Keeps group together and on the same point. Time control is easier. Useful for large group size (20 or more).	Can be dull if used too long without participation. Difficult to determine whether or not people are learning. Retention is limited.

Lesson 6: Selecting Training Methods

Example: Selecting Training Methods

As you recall, Chris's last activity was to outline the training content for the learning objectives in the ethics training.

Note: Take a moment to review Chris's Training Content Outline worksheet, page 3-6 in your Coursebook.

As so often happens, while she was outlining the training content, Chris began thinking about the best training methods to use in teaching that content.

Chris jotted down those thoughts, even though they are preliminary at this time. Later, when Chris develops the training plan, she will select her method.

Table 6-4 on the next page shows Chris's preliminary selection of a training method.

Train-the-Trainer Participant Coursebook

**Table 6-4. Preliminary Selection of
Training Methods for Ethics Training**

Learning Objective: By the end of the lesson, participants will be able to state the ethical standards required by the organization.

    Methods: *Trainer presentation: Trainer presents established ethical standards required by the organization.*

    Structured exercise: Small groups develop responses to customers, suppliers, and employees relative to the organization's ethical standards.

Learning Objective: By the end of the lesson, participants will be able to identify appropriate behavior in circumstances involving ethical issues.

    Methods: *Trainer presentation: Trainer presents factors that define circumstances as ethical situations and appropriate behaviors relative to ethical situations.*

    Case study: Participants read examples of hypothetical situations and identify appropriate and inappropriate behavior relative to ethical issues.

    Group discussion: Participants ask questions about situations they are still unclear about. Ethics expert available to answer difficult questions.

Learning Objective: By the end of the lesson, participants will be able to state correct procedures for reporting instances of ethical violations.

    Methods: *Trainer presentation: Trainer presents reportable ethical violations and reporting procedures.*

    Demonstration: Participants view a video showing correct handling of ethical violations and receive a handout of the reporting steps.

Lesson 6: Selecting Training Methods

Exercise: Selecting Training Methods

The purpose of this exercise is to let you do some preliminary selection of training methods for the training content you outlined in Lesson 5.

Turn to Coursebook page 3-7 and take out your training content outline. Jot down possible training methods you might use in teaching the training content. Refer to Tables 6-1 through 6-3, as needed, to complete this exercise.

PRELIMINARY SELECTION OF TRAINING METHODS

Train-the-Trainer Participant Coursebook

Summary

In this lesson, you learned about six common training methods and some criteria you can use in selecting them for your training. You also made some preliminary selections of training methods for teaching the training content you developed in Lesson 5. When you develop your training plan later in the workshop, you will have an opportunity to return to this preliminary selection and finalize your training methods at that time.

In Lesson 7, you will learn about another important element in training—training aids.

Lesson 7
Developing and Using Training Aids

Contents

Overview	7-1
Lesson Objective	7-1
Developing and Using Training Aids	7-2
Videotape	7-3
Handouts	7-5
Flipcharts	7-7
Slides and Overhead Transparencies	7-9
Exercise: Developing a Training Aid	7-13
Summary	7-14

Overview

This lesson covers another important aspect of training—developing and using training aids to help teach the training content of your lesson. You will learn about four training aids you should consider using in your training. During the lesson, you will develop a training aid for your practice training lesson.

Lesson Objective

By the end of this lesson, you will be able to:

- Develop and use training aids appropriately in training.

Developing and Using Training Aids

Definition and Types of Training Aids

In Lesson 6, you learned that training methods are the approaches you use to teach the content of a lesson. Training aids are the visual and written materials (or some combination of the two) that support the training methods you have chosen.

We will be dealing with five of the most commonly used training aids. They are:

1. Video
2. Handouts
3. Flipcharts
4. Slides
5. Overhead Transparencies

Purposes of Training Aids

Training aids serve a variety of purposes. They are used to:

1. Focus attention on what is being discussed by having participants visually review the material.

2. Increase interest in the topic by presenting material that is visually appealing.

3. Improve participant retention by engaging more than one sense (e.g., hearing and seeing) in the presentation of material.

The following sections will discuss in more detail the four training aids covered in this lesson.

Lesson 7: Developing and Using Training Aids

Video

Video has particular advantages in training. Consider using this training aid to:

1. Stimulate interest.

2. Motivate participants to try new things.

3. Illustrate behaviors, including the depiction of subtle expressions.

4. Add professionalism to your training.

Normally, you will not be developing new videotapes for your training because of the costs involved. However, you might decide to use an already-developed videotape if you find one that is appropriate.

There are four steps to follow in using video most effectively in training. We call the steps "The Four P's." They are:

1. **P**repare the video for showing.
2. **P**review the video and provide instructions to participants.
3. **P**lay the video.
4. **P**resent/summarize the learning points.

Table 7-1 on the next page describes the four steps in more detail.

Table 7-1. Steps for Using Video in Training

STEP	DESCRIPTION
1. Prepare for showing	• Check to see that the tape is the correct size for the available equipment. • View the tape ahead of time and identify the important points you want participants to get from viewing it. • Try out the equipment and check lighting levels. If you will be asking participants to take notes, adjust lighting plans accordingly.
2. Preview and provide instructions	• Tell participants what they will see and why. • Instruct participants on what to do during the video (take notes, watch for certain items, etc.). • Tell participants what they will do after the video (discuss what they saw, complete an exercise, etc.).
3. Play the videotape	• Adjust lighting. • Start videotape and adjust picture and volume. • Monitor participants and their reactions to the video.
4. Present/summarize learning points	• At the end of the videotape, have participants complete the learning activity. • Summarize the key points you want participants to learn from the videotape.

Lesson 7: Developing and Using Training Aids

Handouts

Handouts are written materials prepared in advance and distributed to the participants during the training. The information covered in the handout can be used during the training and/or kept for use after the training.

Handouts are important training aids to consider, particularly if you want to:

1. Have participants use the information at a later time (during the training or after the training).

2. Allow participants to absorb information at their own pace.

3. Eliminate the need for participants to memorize or take notes.

The first step in developing a handout is to decide on the format you will use for presenting the information. One of the choices you have is to present the information in paragraph form. (The information you are reading right now is an example of information in paragraph form.) It has its place in handouts, but it also has its drawbacks.

A major drawback of information in paragraph form is that it is visually less appealing to the reader than in other formats. This is particularly true if you are presenting a lot of information. There are other formats you can use that are more interesting to readers and that do a better job of communicating your information under certain conditions.

Three handout formats that are particularly helpful as training aids are:

1. Decision charts
2. Checklists
3. Worksheets

When you select a format, your decision should be based on what you are trying to accomplish with your handout. Table 7-2 shows some guidelines for you to follow in deciding among the three formats listed above.

Table 7-2. Selecting Handout Formats

If you wish to...	Then consider using...	For example...
Guide participants in making decisions	A decision chart	This chart is a decision chart
Provide memory joggers to help participants carry out a task	A checklist	Table 7-3 below is an example
Provide a means to record information	A worksheet	You used a worksheet to outline your resources and learning goals in Lesson 1 (page 1-5)

Regardless of the handout format you choose, there are certain general guidelines to follow in developing handouts. Table 7-3 below provides those guidelines in a checklist form.

Table 7-3. Guidelines for Developing Handouts

CHECK (✓) WHEN DONE	GUIDELINES
☐	Title the handout and date it.
☐	Identify the purpose of the handout.
☐	Specify when and how the handout is to be used.
☐	Note any additional materials that are needed.
☐	Underline, capitalize, or use bold print to emphasize information.
☐	Arrange information so it's easy to read.
☐	Use short sentences in the active voice.
☐	Avoid unnecessary information.

Lesson 7: Developing and Using Training Aids

Flipcharts

Flipcharts consist of an easel and blank pages that can be written on. The information can be prepared ahead of time, or recorded during training.

Filling out the chart ahead of time is neater and more efficient; recording during training allows you to respond to the immediate learning situation.

Regardless of whether you choose to pre-record flipchart pages or record during training, there are certain general guidelines that should make your flipcharts readable and appealing to participants, as shown in Table 7-4 below.

Table 7-4. Guidelines for Making Flipcharts Readable and Appealing

- Make letters at least 1½ inches high.
- Leave two inches or more between lines.
- Use as few words as possible.
- Highlight key points by using:

    | Color | Graphics | Lines |
    | Shapes | Boxes | Pictures |

- Check readability by going to various parts of the room and assessing whether or not it is legible.
- Leave a blank page between each pre-prepared page so that the writing on the next chart page does not show through and distract participants.

Table 7-5 on the next page provides some additional tips for working with flipcharts.

Table 7-5. Flipchart Tips

IF...	THEN...
If you are recording input:	- Record words quickly. - Check with participants to be sure you are reflecting their ideas accurately. - Alternate colors when listing the group's ideas.
If you wish to have participants compare and contrast data:	- Use two flipcharts.
If you want to display information for a period of time:	- Hang pages on the wall.
If you want to look especially professional in front of the group:	- Lightly write memory joggers in pencil in the margin of the flipchart page, and use presentation notes. - Practice tearing pages cleanly before doing it in front of the group. - Tab specific pages ahead of time. - Cover errors with paste-on labels; then write the correct information on the labels. - Cover flipchart information when it is not being used.

Lesson 7: Developing and Using Training Aids

Slides and Overhead Transparencies

The proper use of slides (such as those created using PowerPoint or Presentations software) and overhead transparencies can help you focus your participants' attention on the material being presented. Slides and overhead transparencies also add an increased level of professionalism when they are well-organized and visually appealing. They can be used to effectively increase learning.

Although slides and overhead transparencies can help make your training more effective, there are drawbacks if they are not used properly. Table 7-6 below highlights the advantages and drawbacks.

Table 7-6. Advantages and Drawbacks of Slides/Overhead Transparencies

ADVANTAGES	DRAWBACKS
• They add a professional touch. • They are easily transported. • They can be used with large audiences (over 25).	• The light and glare can be tiring if slides or transparencies are overused. • They require special equipment that is not always readily available. • If the information presented is too complex, it can overwhelm viewers.

The secret to avoiding problems with slides or transparencies is to plan well. Ideally, slides and transparencies should be developed in advance of the presentation. However, you can develop a transparency yourself by using a transparency marker and writing on a transparency film during the presentation.

Many slides today are developed using PowerPoint or Presentations, so it is simple to add graphics to already-prepared slides. You can also have a professional graphic artist design your slides.

Regardless of whether you are developing the slides or transparencies yourself or developing the information so a professional can create them, there are guidelines to ensure that they are effective.

Table 7-7 on the following page provides guidelines for making slides and overhead transparencies readable and appealing.

Table 7-7. Guidelines for Making Slides and Transparencies Readable and Appealing

1. **Make the text legible.**
   You can test legibility by trying to read it from the back row of your training space.

2. **Keep the text simple. Use as few words as possible to communicate your ideas.**
   - Try to use no more than six or seven lines of text per slide/transparency.
   - Try to use no more than six to seven words per line of text.
   - Cover one major idea, with up to three sub-points, on one slide.

3. **Make it clear.**
   - Develop a title for each slide/transparency.
   - Choose fonts, font sizes, and colors than enhance the readability of your slides/transparencies.
   - Bullet items, rather than use narrative sentences or paragraphs.
   - Use the least number of words possible to convey your ideas.

4. **Illustrate your ideas with:**
   - Pictures
   - Shapes
   - Graphs
   - Colors

Table 7-8 provides some guidelines for using slides or transparencies during training.

Table 7-8. Guidelines for Using Slides or Transparencies

1. During presentation of the slide/transparency, keep the image on the screen only until the audience grasps the meaning.

2. Control attention and avoid distractions by turning the projection equipment off or blanking out the screen image when slides are not being shown.

3. Talk to the audience, not the slide.

4. Avoid blocking the audience's view of the screen.

Lesson 7: Developing and Using Training Aids

The guidelines for presenting written information on a slide or transparency are essentially the same; however, one advantage of using slides is that you can also use animation and sound.

Table 7-9 below provides guidelines for using slides.

Table 7-9. Guidelines for Using Slides

IF . . .	THEN . . .
If you use animation:	• Pick one type of animation and use it every time during the presentation. • Gradually introduce text to the audience. This can be done with a mouse click or by timing the appearance of bulleted items so that they appear automatically. • Pick one primary transition, and stick with it. • Consider animating graphical images when dealing with a complex subject.
If you use transitions:	• Choose one or two non-distracting transitions. • Use a "wipe-up" transition to guide the audience's eyes gracefully back to the top of the presentation. • Fade to black between major sections to signal your audience that a new topic is being addressed. • Consider your audience. In general, subtlety and consistency are best.
If you use sound effects:	• Use sound effects sparingly, and make sure they add impact. • Test the sound at various volume levels.

Table 7-10 on the following page presents guidelines for using transparencies.

Table 7-10. Guidelines for Transparencies

IF . . .	THEN . . .
If you are using more than one transparency:	• Turn the projector on, show a transparency, then turn it off—unless you are showing a series in rapid succession. • Don't keep a transparency on too long. The image becomes tiring for viewers.

If you want the group to focus on a specific area:	• Try one of these methods:
	   – Use a pencil to point to the area. Lay the pencil on the plastic to steady the pointer.
	   – Reveal one area at a time by using a piece of paper to "mask" the areas you don't want showing. Place the paper *between the transparency and the glass* for extra control and to enable you to read the masked information.

If you are using the same transparencies in subsequent sessions:	• Mount transparencies in plastic frames to keep them from curling. • Store them sandwiched between papers in a dust-free location.
If you want to look more professional in front of the group:	• Write memory joggers in black ink on the transparency frames if there is space for notes, or on the papers used to separate the transparencies. Refer to these notes as you speak to the group so that you cover all the points you want to make.

Lesson 7: Developing and Using Training Aids

Exercise: Developing and Using Training Aids

The purpose of this exercise is to give you practice in developing training aids.

Using supplies provided by the trainer, create one or more training aids (handouts, flipchart pages, transparencies) that support the practice-training content you outlined in Lesson 5.

When you have finished, the trainer will ask you to show the training aid(s) you have created and describe how you plan to use your training aids in your lesson.

Summary

In this lesson, you learned about developing and using training aids. You will have the opportunity to use the information you learned in this lesson when you prepare for and conduct your practice-training lesson later in the workshop.

In Lesson 8, you will learn the last skill in the process of developing training—creating the lesson plan.

Lesson 8
Developing a Lesson Plan

Contents

Overview	8-1
Lesson Objective	8-1
Developing a Lesson Plan	8-2
The ROPES Model	8-2
Timing Your Lesson	8-5
Formatting Your Lesson Plan	8-7
Example: Developing a Lesson Plan	8-9
Exercise: Developing a Lesson Plan	8-12
Summary	8-14

Overview

In this lesson, you will learn how to develop a lesson plan. This is when you pull together the training content, training methods, and training aids into a plan you will use to conduct the training.

During this lesson, you will be introduced to the "ROPES" model. This is a model for structuring the lesson so that your participants can learn most effectively. You will see how Chris uses the ROPES model to develop a lesson plan for the ethics training. Then you will practice using the ROPES model to develop the lesson plan for your practice training lesson.

Lesson Objective

By the end of this lesson, you will be able to:

- Develop a lesson plan.

Developing a Lesson Plan

Definition and Purpose

A lesson plan is your written record of how you plan to conduct the training. It includes the training content you have outlined for the learning objective and the training methods and training aids you will use to teach the content.

Your lesson plan serves different purposes at different points in time, as shown below.

1. *During lesson development:*
   It is a planning tool for helping you plan the details of the lesson.

2. *Before conducting the lesson:*
   It is a guide for preparing for and rehearsing the lesson.

3. *During the lesson:*
   It is a roadmap for you to follow in conducting the lesson.

4. *After the lesson:*
   It is a document that you (or others) can revise or use as written to conduct the lesson again.

Regardless of how many times you intend to use the lesson, you need to develop a lesson plan. It helps you make sure that you have provided what the participants need in order to learn, and it enables you to conduct your training in a professional manner.

The ROPES Model

There is more to a lesson than presenting the training content you have outlined. A lesson includes a series of steps designed to help the participants learn and practice new skills.

You will be using a model to help you organize your lesson plan so that it includes all of the steps that help your participants meet their learning objectives. It is called the "ROPES" model. The ROPES model has the following five steps:

- **R** = Review
- **O** = Overview
- **P** = Presentation
- **E** = Exercise
- **S** = Summary

The ROPES model steps are defined in Table 8-1 on the following page.

Lesson 8: Developing a Lesson Plan

Table 8-1. The "ROPES" Model

STEPS	PURPOSE
REVIEW	To conduct a review of the participants' general knowledge of or experience with the topic.
OVERVIEW	To establish a connection between the participants and the training content that engages the participants and motivates them to learn.
PRESENTATION	To present the content to the participants in ways that help them retain the information.
EXERCISE	To enable the participants to practice using the training content in order to build their skills.
SUMMARY	To summarize and clarify what was learned.

Using the ROPES Model to Develop Your Lesson Plan

The ROPES Model provides a systematic approach to developing your lesson plan. Starting with the REVIEW step, plan each of the five ROPES steps. Consider **what** will be covered (the content) and **how** it will be covered (the training methods and training aids) for each step. Use Table 8-2 as a guide for using the ROPES Model to develop your lesson plan.

Table 8-2. Developing Your Lesson Plan

STEPS	DESCRIPTION
1. Develop the REVIEW step.	• Introduce the lesson topic. • Have the participants share their knowledge or past experiences with the topic. • Recognize the potential resources in the group.
2. Develop the OVERVIEW step.	• Summarize the activities that will occur in the lesson. • Cover the learning objective(s). • Establish why it is important for the participants to learn the training content.
3. Develop the PRESENTATION step.	• Cover the training content, using the TELL-then-SHOW approach. TELL the participants what is to be done and how to do it. Then SHOW them how to do it by using examples or a demonstration.
4. Develop the EXERCISE step.	• Have the participants practice their new skills. • Provide feedback on their performance.
5. Develop the SUMMARY step.	• Summarize the lesson, stressing important points. • Answer questions. • Make a transition to the next lesson, if there is one, or discuss how the participants can apply the skills back on the job.

Lesson 8: Developing a Lesson Plan

Timing Your Lesson

Time is a very important consideration in training. Usually you have a limited amount of training time. The time you have available for your lesson makes a difference in the training methods you select for your ROPES steps.

Start with the total time you can allot to the lesson, and then apportion the time across the ROPES steps. A rule of thumb is to allocate more training time to the EXERCISE step (so the participants can practice) than to any other single step. While there are no hard and fast rules for allocating training time, Table 8-3 provides some general guidelines for you to follow.

Table 8-3. Timing Guidelines

ROPES STEP	% OF TOTAL TRAINING TIME
REVIEW	5–10%
OVERVIEW	10–15%
PRESENTATION	25–35%
EXERCISE	35–50%
SUMMARY	5%

After you have completed your lesson plan, check your timing. Try these suggestions:

1. Envision the activities that will occur in each step, and mentally judge the approximate time they will take.

2. Practice your presentations, and time your practices.

3. Ask others to assume the role of your participants, and time them as they perform the participant activities. (Allow extra time for the questions and discussions your "real" participants will generate.)

Make your estimates as accurate as possible, and modify your lesson plan if your estimates are significantly different from your original allotments.

Formatting Your Lesson Plan

A two-column lesson format is an easy format to prepare and use. Table 8-4 shows a two-column format and the suggested content in each column.

Table 8-4. Suggested Format for a Two-Column Lesson Plan

LESSON PLAN OUTLINE	TIME/TRAINING AIDS
An outline of what will occur in each ROPES step should include: • Statements you will make or key points you will cover. • Questions you will ask. • Directions you will follow.	Your time allotment for that step. The training aids you will use, noted in the outline at the time you plan to use them.

The level of detail you include in your lesson plan will be based on your specific needs. Some trainers feel more comfortable using a detailed lesson plan; others prefer an abbreviated outline. As a rule, it's best to start out with a detailed plan. As you establish more confidence, you can always simplify it.

You will see an example of a moderately detailed lesson plan using the two-column format shown above when we return to the hypothetical training situation about ethics.

Lesson 8: Developing a Lesson Plan

Example: Developing a Lesson Plan

Let's continue with the example of the request for ethics training.

As you recall, Chris has outlined the training content for the learning objective and has done some preliminary thinking of the training methods to use in teaching that content. Now Chris is ready to develop the lesson plan for the training.

Chris starts by considering the amount of time available for the training. Since Chris has been given a time limitation of one day for the entire training, she has allotted two hours to each of the first two objectives, and one hour to each of the last two objectives.

Next, Chris plans the ROPES steps for each lesson. She develops each ROPES step, outlining the activities that will be included in each step and the training methods and training aids that will be used. Questions she plans to ask are also noted in the lesson plan.

When the lesson plan is finished, Chris checks the timing and sets a time limit for each step.

Table 8-5 shows Chris's completed lesson plan for **one** of the ethics training lessons.

Table 8-5. Example of Completed Lesson Plan

LESSON PLAN OUTLINE	TIME/TRAINING AIDS
I. Review	10 minutes
A. Introduce the lesson.	
Now we are going to discuss the behavior that is appropriate in circumstances involving ethical issues.	
B. Ask:	
"What are some situations you've encountered where you've been unsure about the appropriate ethical behavior to follow?"	Write situations on flipchart. Post on wall.
II. Overview	5 minutes
A. Provide an overview of the lesson.	
1. *In this lesson, you will learn the factors that define an "ethical situation."*	
2. *You will be working with case examples of ethical situations, identifying appropriate behavior in each.*	
3. *Before this lesson has concluded, you'll have a chance to clarify anything you're still not sure about. We'll be joined by an "expert" who will answer questions.*	
B. Display lesson objective.	Show Slide 1: Lesson 2 Objective.

Table 8-5. Example of Completed Lesson Plan
(continued)

LESSON PLAN OUTLINE	TIME/TRAINING AIDS

C. Ask/discuss:
 	
"Why is it so important for all of us to identify potential ethical compromises and act ethically when we encounter them?"
 	
Answer:
 	
We are putting our jobs and our organizations at risk if we fail to identify and respond appropriately to ethical compromises.
 	
III. Presentation
 	
   A. Present factors defining an "ethical situation."
 	
   B. Present general behaviors appropriate for ethical situations.
 	
   C. Use an example from a flipchart.
 	
      Ask:
 	
      1. *"Which factor(s) does this situation involve?"*
 	
      2. *"What behavior would be appropriate in this situation?"*
 	
IV. Exercise
 	
   A. Distribute handout on case examples.
 	
   B. Divide group into teams.
 	
   C. Have teams complete handout on case examples.
 	
   D. Have groups report conclusions.
	
	Show Slide 2: What Are "Ethical Situations"?
	
	Show Slide 3: Appropriate Behaviors
	
	Refer to flipchart page on wall.
	
	1 hour
	
	Handout #1: Case Examples

Table 8-5. Example of Completed Lesson Plan
(continued)

LESSON PLAN OUTLINE	TIME/TRAINING AIDS

E. Discuss, clarify case example answers.
 	
F. Clarify remaining issues of concern.
 	
    1. Introduce the "expert."
 	
    2. Discuss remaining flipchart situations.
 	
    3. Facilitate final question-and-answer session with expert.
 	
V. Summary
 	
A. Summarize lesson.
 	
B. Make the transition to the next lesson.
 	
    1. *Our next lesson will deal with how to report ethical violations.*
 	
    2. *Following correct reporting procedures is another critical aspect of dealing appropriately with ethical situations.*
	Refer to flipchart page on wall.
	
	5 minutes
	
	Show Slide 4: Lesson 2 Summary

Lesson 8: Developing a Lesson Plan

Exercise: Developing a Lesson Plan

The purpose of this exercise is to give you practice in developing a lesson plan. You will use the lesson plan you develop in this exercise to conduct a segment of your practice training lesson in Lesson 11.

Take out the training content outline you developed in Lesson 5 (Coursebook page 5-8).

Your instructor will be providing blank lesson plan formats for you to use in developing your lesson plan. Indicate on your lesson plan the points at which you will be using training aids; however, do not develop your training aids yet. As you draft your lesson plan, leave space for making changes or additions to your plan.

Refer to the following tables for help in developing your lesson plan:

- Table 8-2, page 8-4
- Table 8-3, page 8-5
- Table 8-5, pages 8-8 through 8-10

Your instructor will be available to consult with you during this exercise.

Train-the-Trainer Participant Coursebook

Summary

In this lesson, you learned how to develop a training plan. You will use the training plan you developed when you conduct your practice training later in the workshop.

Lesson 9 begins the fourth step in the training process—conducting the training. In that lesson, you will learn the delivery skills associated with facilitating learning.

Lesson 9
Using Basic Facilitation Skills

Contents

Overview	9-1
Lesson Objectives	9-1
Using Basic Facilitation Skills	9-2
Types of Facilitation Skills	9-2
Attending Skills	9-3
Observing Skills	9-4
Exercise 1: Using Observing Skills	9-6
Listening Skills	9-8
Exercise 2: Using Listening Skills	9-10
Questioning Skills	9-11
Exercise 3: Using Questioning Skills	9-17
Exercise 4: Building Questions into Training	9-19
Summary	9-20

Overview

This lesson covers a key aspect of conducting training—using basic facilitation skills. You will learn four basic facilitation skills that you can use in conducting training. During the lesson you will see these skills demonstrated, and you will have a chance to practice using them. At the end of the lesson, you will return to your lesson plan and build in opportunities for using facilitation skills during your training.

Lesson Objectives

By the end of this lesson, you will be able to:

- Make accurate observations.
- Demonstrate listening skills through paraphrasing.
- Use appropriate questioning techniques.

Using Basic Facilitation Skills

Definition and Purpose

Adults learn best when they participate in the training process. When you use facilitation skills, you encourage involvement by showing interest in the participants and allowing them to feel free to comment and ask questions. Facilitation skills also help you to obtain feedback from the participants about how the training is being received. This enables you to respond to their needs most appropriately.

Facilitation skills, then, help you bridge the gap between the training content and the participants, as shown in Figure 9-1 below.

Figure 9-1. Purpose of Facilitation Skills

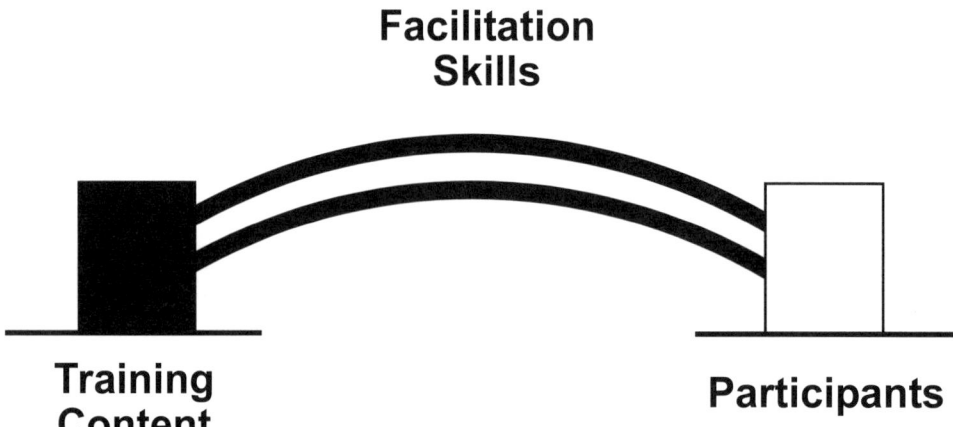

Types of Facilitation Skills

You will use four basic facilitation skills in conducting your training. They are:

1. Attending
2. Observing
3. Listening
4. Questioning

The following sections will discuss these four skills in detail.

Lesson 9: Using Basic Facilitation Skills

Attending Skills

Attending means presenting yourself physically in a manner that shows you are paying attention to participants. When you use attending skills, you are building rapport with them. You are communicating that you value them as individuals and are interested in their learning.

Attending helps you gather information from participants. Your physical positioning enables you to observe people's behavior, an important source of information in assessing how the training is being received. It also encourages participants to interact verbally with you.

There are four attending behaviors that show you are interested in participants. They are:

1. Facing the participants.
2. Maintaining appropriate eye contact.
3. Moving toward the participants.
4. Avoiding behavior that distracts.

Table 9-1 below provides some guidelines for you to follow in using attending skills.

Table 9-1. Guidelines for Using Attending Skills

Do	Don't
• Position your body so you face all participants. • Continually scan the group with your eyes. • Walk toward people. • Smile at individuals. • Nod affirmatively. • Circle the room during exercises to check participants' progress. • Use natural facial expressions in talking with participants.	• Don't talk to visual aids. • Don't turn your back to part of the group. • Don't stare at individuals. • Don't avoid making eye contact and don't scan the group too frequently or too rapidly. • Don't put too much distance between you and your participants. • Don't stand in a fixed position. • Don't shuffle papers or look at your watch while people are talking.

Observing Skills

Observing skills help you assess how the training is being received. Based on your observations, you can make decisions to continue the learning process as planned, or to modify it in response to participant needs.

There are three steps in using observation skills:

Step 1: Look at the person's face, body position, and body movements.

Is the person smiling? Frowning? Nodding? Yawning? Looking at you? Looking away?

Step 2: Try to determine the person's feelings, based on what you have observed.

Step 3: Take appropriate action based on the inferences made.

Table 9-2 below provides a list of nonverbal behaviors and some inferences you might make about the participants' feelings when you observe them.

Table 9-2. Participants' Nonverbal Behaviors and Their Possible Feelings

BEHAVIORS	POSSIBLE FEELINGS
Smiling Nodding affirmatively Leaning forward Making eye contact	Enthusiasm/Understanding
Yawning Vacant stare Shuffling feet Leaning back in chair Looking at clock	Boredom
Frowning Scratching head Pursing lips Vacant stare Avoiding eye contact	Confusion

Although a single behavior can serve as an indicator of a feeling, your inferences will be based on all your observations. Whether you decide to take action or not will depend on the situation as you view it—how many people are experiencing the feeling, the depth and possible duration of it, the impact it will have on present and future learning, etc. If the situation warrants action in your judgment, consider the possible actions shown in Table 9-4 on the next page.

Table 9-4. Responding to Participant Behavior

IF THE INFERENCE YOU DRAW IS...	AND...	THEN...
Enthusiasm/ Understanding	• Several participants display the behavior	• Continue, and make a mental note that the training is being well-received.
	• One participant displays the behavior	• Continue, and make a mental note to check again later.
Boredom	• Several participants display the behavior	• Try taking a break, speeding up, or checking your training method to be sure that the participants are involved in the training process.
	• One participant displays the behavior	• Continue, but make a mental note to reassess later.
Confusion	• Several participants display the behavior	• Ask participants about areas of confusion, and provide clarification by giving examples or rephrasing information.
	• One participant displays the behavior	• Ask participant about areas of confusion and provide clarification. If time is limited, talk with the person at the next break.

Train-the-Trainer Participant Coursebook

Exercise 1: Using Observing Skills

The purpose of this exercise is to give you a chance to observe some typical non-verbal behaviors displayed by participants, and to make inferences about what the participants might be feeling.

Your instructor will be asking a few members of the group to exhibit specific non-verbal behaviors while you observe them. Using the worksheet on the following page:

1. List what you observe about the person's face, body position, and body movements.

2. Jot down the feelings you infer, based on the behaviors you have observed.

There will be a group discussion after each example.

Lesson 9: Using Basic Facilitation Skills

Exercise 1: Using Observing Skills (concluded)

Example 1

Behaviors Observed: _____
_____
_____

Inferred Feelings: _____
_____
_____

Example 2

Behaviors Observed: _____
_____
_____

Inferred Feelings: _____
_____
_____

Example 3

Behaviors Observed: _____
_____
_____

Inferred Feelings: _____
_____
_____

Listening Skills

Listening, as we define it, means obtaining verbal information and verifying that you understand the information. Listening skills enable you to demonstrate your understanding of the person's perspective. They also provide you with feedback about how the training is being received. You can use this feedback in considering how you need to proceed in conducting your training.

Listening involves two key steps. They are:

1. **Listening to the words being expressed,** which means maintaining concentration on what the person is saying.

2. **Paraphrasing what was said to demonstrate understanding,** which means interacting with the person to ensure that you accurately understand the person's information.

Each of these steps is discussed in more detail below.

Step 1: Listen to the words being expressed.

As you listen to the words being expressed, try to grasp both the content and the meaning of the words from the participant's perspective. While this may sound simple, you will find that the major roadblocks to listening to the person's words are the internal and external distractions that compete with good listening habits.

Internal distractions are the competing thoughts that develop inside you while the person is talking. Sometimes they are related to what the person is saying; sometimes they are mental excursions to unrelated topics. You must eliminate these internal distractions that keep you from focusing on what the participant is saying.

External distractions are things that happen in the learning environment that compete with your attention on the participant. They can be sights or sounds. Exclude them or at least put them out of your mind until the person has finished speaking.

Once you have focused on the person's message, you can then proceed to the next step—demonstrating your understanding of what the person said.

Step 2: Paraphrase what was said to demonstrate understanding.

Paraphrasing to demonstrate understanding requires you to verbally interact with the participant. The interaction is either to:

- Get additional information you're missing.

- Verify with the participant what you think was said.

Use a phrase such as "You're saying . . .," or "As I understand it . . ." before paraphrasing what the participant said. If you then paraphrase the information accurately, the person can confirm that you have demonstrated understanding. If you paraphrase inaccurately or miss important details, the person can add the information needed for you to understand.

Exercise 2: Using Listening Skills

The purpose of this exercise is to give you a chance to practice using listening skills.

Your instructor will read three statements that might be made by participants. Using the worksheet below, paraphrase what you believe was said.

There will be a group discussion after each statement; volunteers will share their statements with the class.

Example 1

Your paraphrase statement: _____
_____
_____
_____

Example 2

Your paraphrase statement: _____
_____
_____
_____

Example 3

Your paraphrase statement: _____
_____
_____
_____

Lesson 9: Using Basic Facilitation Skills

Questioning Skills

Questions play a major role in training. Questions can:

- Help you determine what the participants already know about a topic, so you can focus your training on what they need to learn.

- Invite participation and involvement in the training process.

- Provide you with feedback about how the training is being received.

- Enable your participants to evaluate what they know and don't know, and fill in the gaps.

There are three skills associated with the questioning process. They are:

1. Asking questions.

2. Handling answers to questions.

3. Responding to questions.

Each of these will be explored in more detail below.

Asking Questions

Asking effective questions is one of the most important skills you can develop. Asking effective questions means selecting the right **type** of question, **phrasing** it so it elicits the response you are after, and then **directing** the question appropriately.

Types of Questions

There are two basic types of questions from which to choose—**open** questions and **closed** questions.

Table 9-5 gives a brief description and an example of each type.

Table 9-5. Types of Questions

TYPE OF QUESTION	DESCRIPTION	EXAMPLE
Open	<ul><li>Requires more than a *yes* or *no* or one-word answer.</li><li>Stimulates thinking.</li><li>Elicits discussion.</li><li>Usually begins with *what, how, when,* or *why*.</li></ul>	*What ideas do you have for explaining the changes to our clients?*
Closed	<ul><li>Requires a one-word answer.</li><li>Closes off discussion.</li><li>Usually begins with *is, can, how many, does*.</li></ul>	*Does everyone understand the changes we've discussed?*

Lesson 9: Using Basic Facilitation Skills

Phrasing Questions

Once you have decided on the type of question you will use, you need to determine how you will phrase it. There are important considerations in phrasing questions so that participants are focused on the precise information you are trying to obtain. Table 9-6 provides some guidelines for you to use in phrasing your question.

Table 9-6. Guidelines for Phrasing Questions

Do	Don't
Ask clear, concise questions covering a single issue.	Don't ask rambling, ambiguous questions covering multiple issues.
Ask reasonable questions based on what the participants can be expected to know at this point in the training.	Don't ask questions that are too difficult for the majority of the participants to answer.
Ask challenging questions that require thought.	Don't ask questions that are too easy and that provide no opportunity for thinking.
Ask honest, relevant questions that direct the participants to logical answers.	Don't ask "trick" questions designed to fool the participants.

Directing Questions

The final consideration in asking effective questions is how to direct your question. There are two ways to direct questions:

1. To the group.
2. To a specific individual.

Table 9-7 provides a chart to help you decide how to direct your questions.

Table 9-7. Choosing How to Direct Questions

IF YOU WANT TO...	THEN...
Stimulate all participants to think Allow individuals to respond voluntarily Avoid putting an individual on the spot	Direct the question to the group. **Example:** *What experiences have you had on this issue?*
Stimulate **one** person to think and respond Tap the known resources of an "expert" in the class	Direct the question to an individual. **Example:** *Mary, you have had a lot of experience in applying these regulations with clients. What would you do in this case?*

Lesson 9: Using Basic Facilitation Skills

Handling Answers to Questions

The second skill associated with the questioning process involves the way in which you handle response to your questions. To ensure maximum learning, you need maximum participation. The way in which you respond to a participant's answer has an impact not only on that individual but also on the amount of future participation you will receive from all participants.

Some ways to handle responses and still maintain a high level of participant participation are to:

- Use positive reinforcement for correct answers.

- Acknowledge the effort of the respondent, regardless of whether the answer was right or wrong.

- Minimize potential embarrassment for wrong or incomplete answers.

Table 9-8 provides some tips on handling responses to your questions.

Table 9-8. Tips for Handling Responses

IF THE PARTICIPANT'S RESPONSE IS . . .		
CORRECT	**INCORRECT**	**PARTLY CORRECT**
Use positive reinforcement. **Examples:** *Yes.* *Good point.* *That's right.*	Acknowledge the effort. **Then** Redirect the question to others or answer it yourself. **Examples:** *I can see how you might come up with that. Who else has an idea?* *That's not exactly what I was looking for. What I was looking for was ___.*	Reinforce the correct portion. **Then** Redirect the question to the same person or to another person, or answer it yourself. **Examples:** *You're on the right track. What other ideas do you have?* *That's one good point, Joe. Who else has some ideas?*

Responding to Questions

The third skill associated with the questioning process involves responding to questions from the group. Questions provide an opportunity to enhance the entire group's learning, as well as that of the individual asking the question. The way in which you respond to questions also affects whether participants feel free to ask future questions during training.

There are three acceptable ways to respond to questions. They are:

1. Provide the answer yourself.
2. Redirect the question to a participant.
3. Defer the question.

Table 9-9 provides guidelines for deciding on the appropriate response.

Table 9-9. Responding to Questions

CHOOSE THE FOLLOWING RESPONSE...	WHEN...
Provide the answer yourself.	You are the only person who can provide the answer.
Redirect the question back to the same person, or to another person.	There is a high probability that the person will be able to come up with the correct answer.
Defer the question.	The question is beyond the scope of the course. The question cannot be handled in the allotted time frame. The answer will be provided by material covered later in the course. You need time to get the correct answer and get back to the participant.

Lesson 9: Using Basic Facilitation Skills

Exercise 3: Using Questioning Skills

The purpose of this exercise is to give you practice using questioning skills. The worksheet on the next page presents three typical classroom situations. Respond to each situation and write your responses on the worksheet. Refer to Tables 9-5 through 9-9 for help in completing your responses.

A group discussion will follow the exercise and volunteers will be asked to share their responses with the class.

Exercise 3: Using Questioning Skills (concluded)

Situation 1:

You are using the ROPES model for conducting training and are in the REVIEW portion of your training. You have just introduced the topic of the training, **Conducting Effective Meetings.** You want to find out your participants' knowledge of or experience with the topic.

Develop a question that will accomplish your goal:

_____
_____
_____
_____
_____

Situation 2:

During your training on how to conduct effective meetings, you ask that the participants name the three critical elements you presented earlier in connection with planning effective meetings. One person volunteers one of the elements, *developing the agenda.*

Develop your response:

_____
_____
_____
_____
_____

Situation 3:

In your **Conducting Effective Meetings** course, a participant asks, *"How can I stop a discussion of an agenda item that is going on too long?"*

Develop your response:

_____
_____
_____
_____
_____

Lesson 9: Using Basic Facilitation Skills

Exercise 4: Building Questions Into Training

The purpose of this practice exercise is to give you the opportunity to build questions into your lesson plan to involve the participants.

Review your lesson plan to include additional questions or to improve the questions you planned to ask. Pay particular attention to the REVIEW and PRESENTATION sections of your plan. Record your new or revised questions on your lesson plan at the point where you will ask them.

There will be a brief discussion of this exercise after you finish.

Summary

In this lesson, you learned the four basic facilitation skills used in conducting training. You will have an opportunity to use these skills when you conduct your practice training later in the workshop.

In Lesson 10, you will learn about handling problems that can arise during training.

Lesson 10
Handling Problem Situations

Contents

Overview	10-1
Lesson Objective	10-1
Handling Problem Situations	10-2
Three Essential Considerations	10-2
Identifying Strategies for Handling Problem Situations	10-3
Exercise: Identifying Strategies for Handling Problem Situations	10-4
Summary	10-5

Overview

This lesson covers ways to handle problem situations that can arise during training. You will learn about three key considerations. During the lesson, you will have a chance to practice identifying strategies for handling some common problem situations.

Lesson Objective

By the end of this lesson, you will be able to:

- Identify strategies for resolving common problem situations.

Handling Problem Situations

Problem situations, as we are defining them in this lesson, are those in which **learning is inhibited due to the behavior of one or more of the participants.** All trainers, even the most skilled and experienced ones, occasionally run into problem situations.

As you recall, learning is most likely to take place when people are actively involved and participating in the training process. The basic facilitation skills you learned during Lesson 9 will serve to encourage participation. Frequently, however, problem situations have to do with the **level** of participation of individuals.

Some differences in levels of participation are a natural reflection of variations in personalities and preferred ways of learning. A problem situation occurs, however, when people participate too much or too little.

If individuals are **too vocal**, then others might not be able to participate fully in the training. You might also run out of time before you complete all your training activities.

If individuals are **too silent**, their valuable input is lost from the group. Silent people pose another problem for you—you might have difficulty assessing whether or not they are learning.

Don't assume that problem behavior is a reflection of participants' hostility toward you or your training. Overly vocal individuals might simply be very enthusiastic and excited about the course material, and silent people might just be nervous about expressing themselves in front of the group.

When learning appears inhibited, however, you must take action. By eliminating barriers to learning, you maintain the control over the learning environment necessary if participants are to achieve the learning objectives.

Three Essential Considerations

As the trainer, you are responsible for handling problem situations that are negatively affecting learning. There are three key considerations in handling problem situations. They are shown in Table 10-1 on the next page.

Lesson 10: Handling Problem Situations

Table 10-1. Essential Considerations for Handling Problem Situations

CONSIDERATION	DESCRIPTION
Eliminate or minimize the problem behavior.	You need to resolve the problem to the extent necessary for learning to resume unhindered.
Protect the self-esteem of the person.	You need to take care of the problem in a way that doesn't reduce the self-esteem of the person exhibiting the problem behavior.
Avoid further disruption to learning.	You need to preserve a learning climate that is relaxed, comfortable, and conducive to learning.

Identifying Strategies for Handling Problem Situations

When you are confronted with a problem situation, it is important to remain as emotionally neutral as possible, so that you can identify the best strategies for handling the situation. Use a rational problem-solving approach such as the one described in the three-step model below:

Step 1: Identify *possible* strategies—those you have seen other trainers use, as well as those you think would fit the situation.

Step 2: Evaluate them against the three considerations discussed above, eliminating those that do not meet all three conditions.

Step 3: Select a strategy to use in handling the problem.

Exercise: Identifying Strategies for Handling Problem Situations

The purpose of this exercise is to give you an opportunity to practice identifying strategies for handling a problem situation.

Your trainer will divide the class into two teams. Each team will be asked to identify strategies for dealing with one of the problem situations listed below.

Situation 1: Bill monopolizes the discussions and answers all questions the instructor asks before anyone else has a chance to speak. He tends to wander off the point and tell "war stories."

Situation 2: Jill is constantly interrupting to challenge the trainer on technical details of the course. Her information is usually accurate and shows she has extensive knowledge and experience in the subject.

Wait for your trainer to give your team its assignment. Then, as a team, discuss your assigned problem situation and:

1. Identify possible strategies for handling the problem.

2. Evaluate each strategy against the three conditions listed below, eliminating strategies that do not meet all three conditions.

    - Will it eliminate or minimize the problem behavior?

    - Will it protect the self-esteem of the person whose behavior is causing the problem?

    - Will it avoid further disruption to learning?

Have your team's list of strategies recorded on a flipchart page, and select a spokesperson to report your strategies to the total group.

Lesson 10: Handling Problem Situations

Summary

In this lesson, you learned how to identify ways to handle problem situations. You learned the three key considerations in handling problem situations, and you practiced identifying strategies to solve common problem situations. You can use the approach you learned in this lesson to handle similar problem situations you encounter in conducting training back on the job.

In Lesson 11, you will complete your final preparations and conduct a segment of the lesson plan you have developed during the workshop.

Lesson 11 Practice Training

Contents

Overview	11-1
Lesson Objective	11-1
Putting Yourself at Ease Before Training	11-2
Final Preparations for the Practice Training	11-3
Exercise: Practice Training	11-4
Summary	11-7

Overview

This is the point where you pull together all of the skills you have learned so far in this workshop.

In this lesson, you will complete your final preparations and conduct a segment of your lesson plan.

Lesson Objective

By the end of this lesson, you will be able to:

- Conduct training using your lesson plan.

Putting Yourself at Ease Before Training

Almost everyone who trains feels nervous before training. Most people report that their "trainer nerves" reach their peak just before the training starts.

Table 11-1 provides tips that can help you feel more at ease before training. They include strategies you can employ well ahead of the training, as well as those that can get you through those last minute anxieties.

Table 11-1. Tips for Putting Yourself at Ease Before Training

1. Rehearse until you feel comfortable with your lesson plan.

2. Memorize the words you will say during the first few minutes of your training.

3. Check your training materials and practice using training aids in advance of the training.

4. Anticipate potential problems and prepare to resolve them, should they occur.

5. Get as much rest as possible the night before the training.

6. Select clothing you feel particularly comfortable in for conducting your training.

7. Try putting yourself in your participants' shoes. Consider how uncomfortable people feel at the beginning of the training.

8. Just before beginning to train, relax by:

    - Taking a couple of deep breaths and blowing them out slowly through your mouth.

    - Saying something encouraging to yourself, such as *"It's going to be a good session, and I'm going to enjoy it."*

9. Accept nervousness as an energizer that helps keep you on your toes and performing at your best.

10. Rely on the most powerful training tool you have—your own unique style, experiences, and abilities as a person.

Lesson 11: Practice Training

Final Preparations for the Practice Training

This workshop has concentrated on skills basic to developing and conducting training programs. Soon you will have an opportunity to apply these skills, by conducting a 15-minute segment of the lesson plan you have developed.

At this time, you will complete your final preparations for conducting your training. Follow the steps shown below in preparing for your practice training.

Step 1: Review your lesson plan to determine your 15-minute practice training segment.

Step 2: Develop your training aids for the segment of training you will be conducting. Consider developing training aids that go beyond what you expect to use in 15 minutes, in case you cover more content than you had estimated. Develop any handouts first, and give them to your trainer so that they can be duplicated.

Step 3: Rehearse the segment you will be conducting so that you have a clear idea of what you and the participants will be doing throughout your session. Practice using the visual aids you will be using in the training.

Exercise: Practice Training

The purpose of this exercise is to give you a chance to practice conducting the training you developed for this workshop.

You will be assuming two "roles" during the practice training session: the role of "trainer" when you are conducting your own training segment, and the role of "participant" for other practice trainers. The following chart identifies the responsibilities for each of your roles.

TRAINER ROLE	PARTICIPANT ROLE
Before the training: Come up to the front of the room and organize your training materials. Tell the participants who they are, including any special knowledge/experience they are to assume.	Review the trainer's **Learning Goals** posted on the flipchart, so you can take them into account in providing feedback. Understand the participant role you are to assume.
During the training: Practice the skills you learned in the workshop as you complete your training segment.	Respond to the training as a participant, but pay attention to the training skills the trainer is practicing. Don't "overplay" your role.
After the training: Return to your seat, participate in the feedback discussion, and receive the completed feedback forms from your participants.	Complete your feedback form, participate in the feedback discussion, and give your completed form to the trainer.

Table 11-2 shows the feedback form that will be used in the feedback discussions.

Figure 11-3 provides guidelines on giving and receiving feedback during the discussion sessions that follow the practice training.

Lesson 11: Practice Training

Table 11-2. Feedback Form

Name of Practice Trainer: _____

1. Were appropriate training methods used?

   ❏ Case study ❏ Structured exercise ❏ Demonstration
   ❏ Trainer presentation ❏ Group discussion ❏ Role play

   Notes: _____

2. Were training aids developed and used appropriately?

   Notes: _____

3. Did the trainer use effective attending skills?

   ❏ Facing participants ❏ Moving toward participants
   ❏ Maintaining eye contact ❏ Avoiding distractions

   Notes: _____

4. Did the trainer demonstrate effective listening skills by paraphrasing?

   Notes: _____

5. Did the trainer demonstrate effective questioning skills?

   ❏ Asking questions ❏ Handling participant answers
   ❏ Responding to participant questions

   Notes:

6. Were adult learning principles followed?

   Notes:

7. One thing I particularly liked:

   _____

8. One suggestion I have is:

   _____

Figure 11-3. Guidelines for Sharing Feedback

GUIDELINE	EXPLANATION
GIVING FEEDBACK . . .	
Be specific.	Describe *what you saw* and *how you were affected*.
Be constructive.	Suggest *ways to improve* or other ideas to consider.
Be positive.	Provide examples of what the person did that you liked.
Be concise.	Provide data not already provided by others.
RECEIVING FEEDBACK . . .	
Listen openly.	Don't reject, block the information, or feel you have to "explain."
Understand it.	*Ask for clarification* if you're not sure what is meant.
Analyze it.	Give yourself time to *think about the feedback,* and make decisions later to change/not change.

Lesson 11: Practice Training

Summary

In this lesson, you conducted a training session based on the lesson plan you developed during the workshop. You received feedback on your practice training segment from the viewpoint of your participants. You also served as a participant during training sessions presented by other group members, and provided feedback to them.

In Lesson 12, you will consider ways to evaluate your training to assess its effectiveness.

Lesson 12
Evaluating Training

Contents

Overview	12-1
Lesson Objective	12-1
Evaluating Training	12-2
Benefits of Course Evaluation Data	12-2
Evaluation Levels	12-3
Example: Reaction Level Evaluation	12-5
Example: Learning Level Evaluation	12-6
Data Collection Methods	12-7
Evaluation Steps	12-8
Exercise: Developing a Training Evaluation Plan	12-9
Tips for Conducting Evaluations	12-10
Summary	12-11

Overview

This lesson focuses on the importance of training evaluation. A well-planned and appropriately administered evaluation can benefit the organization and individuals significantly. The organization can ensure that its goals for the training are being met. Future participants can benefit from improvements made as a result of an evaluation. And, as the trainer, the feedback generated from an evaluation can help you become even more effective in your training role.

During this lesson, you will learn about four levels of evaluation. You will see examples of course evaluations that target specific levels. You will also have a chance to do some preliminary evaluation planning.

Lesson Objective

By the end of this lesson, you will be able to:

- Plan an evaluation.

Evaluating Training

Definition and Purpose

A training evaluation is an objective summary of data you gather about the effectiveness of your training. The primary purpose for gathering evaluation data is to make decisions. Training evaluations help you (and others) decide whether the training is accomplishing its goals. They also help you decide how to modify your approaches for greater effectiveness.

Benefits of Course Evaluation Data

When you have training evaluation data, you are able to make judgments about:

- How well the training met the training needs identified.
- How well the participants mastered the training content.
- Whether the training methods and media helped participants achieve the instructional objectives.
- How much of the training transferred to the work setting.
- Whether the training contributed to the achievement of the organization's goals.
- Whether the benefits derived from the training justified the cost of the training.

Lesson 12: Evaluating Training

Evaluation Levels

There are four levels of training evaluations, each measuring a different outcome of training. The four levels are:

1. Reaction
2. Learning
3. Behavior
4. Results

The level you choose depends upon the data you wish to develop, as shown below.

> **Reaction:** Training evaluations can provide data on how the participants reacted to the training content, training activities, instructor, and any other important aspect of the training.
>
> **Learning:** Training evaluations can provide data on the knowledge participants gained during the training course.
>
> **Behaviors:** Training evaluations can provide data on the new behaviors used by participants when they return to their work settings.
>
> **Results:** Training evaluations can provide data on how the training impacted organizational goals.

The general evaluation questions answered by each of the four levels and the types of information typically collected during each level are shown in Table 12-1. Examples of Course Evaluations for levels one and two are shown on pages 12-5 and 12-6.

Table 12-1. Levels of Evaluation

LEVELS	EVALUATION QUESTIONS	TYPES OF INFORMATION COLLECTED
Reaction	Were the participants pleased with the course?	Participant impressions of . . . ❑ Instructors ❑ Course materials ❑ Training activities ❑ Training content ❑ Training facilities Observer assessments of how the participants reacted to the training.
Learning	What did the participants learn during the course?	Measurements of what the participants know or can do at the beginning and end of training.
Behaviors	Did the participants change their on-the-job behaviors based on what they learned?	Participant, co-worker, and supervisor impressions of... ❑ Changes in the on-the-job behaviors used by the participants following training Measurements of actual on-the-job behaviors. Observer assessments of changes in on-the-job performance.
Results	Did the change in participant behaviors have a positive impact on the organization?	Participant, supervisor, and/or management impressions of the benefits derived from the training. Measurements of return-on-investment resulting from the training.

Lesson 12: Evaluating Training

Example: Reaction-Level Evaluation

Course Title: _____ **Date:** _____

Rate the QUALITY of each factor listed below, using the following scale:

- (NA) = Not Applicable
- (1) = Unacceptable
- (2) = Needs Improvement
- (3) = Satisfactory
- (4) = Good
- (5) = Excellent

COMMENTS

TRAINING MATERIALS
- ( ) Audio/visual media _____
- ( ) Participant materials _____
- ( ) Activities/exercises _____

CONTENT
- ( ) Training objectives _____
- ( ) Lesson content _____
- ( ) Activities/exercises _____

TRAINER TECHNIQUES
- ( ) Delivery methods _____
- ( ) Assistance provided _____
- ( ) Questions answered _____

Rate the PACE/TIMING using (F) = Fast, (S) = Slow, (JR) = Just Right

COMMENTS

- ( ) Modules
- ( ) Activities/exercises
- ( ) Trainer presentations
- ( ) Other

Train-the-Trainer Participant Coursebook

Example: Learning-Level Evaluation

Course Title: _____ **Date:** _____

For each of the four areas covered by the course, indicate:

- How much you knew about the area BEFORE the course.
- How much you know NOW about the area.
- How VALUABLE you think having the knowledge/skill in the area will be to you.

Assign a rating of 0 to 9 for each of the three questions, using the scale below:

```
    0        | 1   2   3 | 4   5   6 | 7   8   9
Nothing/No Value  A Little      Some        A Lot
```

KNEW BEFORE	KNOW NOW	COURSE AREA	VALUE
		1. **Interpersonal Influence** – Sources of influence – Use of interpersonal influence on the job – Key actions for building interpersonal influence	
		2. **Individual Differences** – Understanding own/others' styles – Special strengths of each style – Flexing your style for increased effectiveness	
		3. **Communication Skills** – Active Listening Skills – Reacting to Ideas of Others – Proposing Own Ideas	
		4. **Meeting Leadership** – Elements of effective meetings – Leadership responsibilities – Meeting preparation – Interactive meetings – Handling "problem participants"	

Lesson 12: Evaluating Training

Data Collection Methods

There are many data collection methods you can use in evaluating your training. Table 12-4 shows examples of data collection methods and the evaluation levels with which they are most likely to be associated.

Table 12-4. Evaluation Methods

EVALUATION METHODS	EVALUATION LEVELS				TYPE OF DATA	
	Reaction	Learning	Behaviors	Results	Objective	Subjective
Questionnaire	✓	✓	✓	✓		✓
Focus Group		✓				✓
Writing Test		✓			✓	✓
Performance Test		✓	✓		✓	✓
Interview	✓	✓	✓	✓		✓
Observation	✓		✓		✓	✓
Performance Records			✓	✓	✓	✓

Evaluation Steps

The following steps are used to conduct a training evaluation:

Step 1: Develop a Training Evaluation Plan

- Select the evaluation level(s):

    Reaction: Were the participants pleased with the course?

    Learning: What did the participants learn during the course?

    Behaviors: Did the participants change their on-the-job behaviors based on what they learned?

    Results: Did the changes in participant behavior have a positive impact on the organization?

- Determine the data to be collected.

- Identify the data collection sources and methods.

Step 2: Collect and Analyze the Data

- Develop the data collection procedures and instruments.

- Develop a data analysis plan.

- Collect the evaluation data.

- Analyze the data.

Step 3: Report the Evaluation Results

- Develop conclusions and recommendations based on analysis of the training data.

- Draft a training evaluation report.

- Present the report to key decision makers and other interested parties.

Lesson 12: Evaluating Training

Exercise: Developing a Training Evaluation Plan

The purpose of this exercise is to give you practice in considering the elements required for an evaluation of your training.

Select one of the four evaluation levels and use it on the worksheet below to do some preliminary planning for this evaluation.

Training Evaluation Plan Worksheet

Evaluation level(s) to be addressed:

    [ ] Reaction   [ ] Learning   [ ] Behaviors   [ ] Results

Important data to gather:

_____

_____

_____

Data source(s):

_____

_____

_____

Data collection method(s) to be used:

    [ ] Questionnaire   [ ] Interview
    [ ] Focus Group   [ ] Observation
    [ ] Written Test   [ ] Performance Records
    [ ] Performance Test

Next steps:

_____

_____

_____

_____

Tips for Conducting Evaluations

Tip 1: Concentrate your efforts on the most important measures.

Put your energy into collecting information that has the greatest potential return. Identify the evaluation data that will provide the most useful information. Then limit your data collection to what will help you get that information.

Tip 2: Use sampling techniques.

Use representative samples of participants or other sources to cut evaluation costs. Then, if necessary, verify key findings from your samples through surveys of larger groups.

Tip 3: Use existing data collection tools.

Modify existing data collection tools used in your organization to develop additional training evaluation information. Or take a data collection form used in a different organization and modify it to meet your needs.

Tip 4: Keep your communication channels open.

Use every opportunity possible to collect information about your training course. Develop informal networks of participants and other personnel to obtain feedback on your classes. Make it easy for people to give you feedback on your training.

Lesson 12: Evaluating Training

Summary

In this lesson, you considered the importance of evaluating your own training, and the potential effects or consequences of not evaluating. You have learned about four levels of evaluation, and you have done some preliminary planning on how you might use one of those levels.

In the final lesson, Lesson 13, you will consider ways to use all of the skills learned in this workshop when you return to your job.

Lesson 13
Using the Training Skills

Contents

Overview 13-1
Lesson Objective 13-1
Workshop Evaluation Form 13-2

Overview

This lesson is intended to provide an opportunity for you to consider what you have learned in the workshop and how you might apply those new skills back at your job.

During this lesson, you will review the objectives for this workshop and the topics that have been covered. You will also familiarize yourself with the final section at the back of the Coursebook.

The Job Aids section contains charts summarizing key ideas from the workshop, as well as blank worksheets you can reproduce and use in preparing training.

After reviewing this section, you will have a chance to discuss what you have learned and the opportunities you see for using your newly acquired skills.

Finally, there will be a short closing exercise, and you will be asked to complete an evaluation form for the workshop.

Lesson Objective

By the end of this lesson, you will be able to:

- Identify ways to transfer your newly acquired training skills to the work setting.

Train-the-Trainer Participant Coursebook

Workshop Evaluation Form

Course Title: _____

Location: _____ **Dates:** _____

PART 1

For each of the topics listed below, circle a number on the **left** to indicate how prepared you felt to accomplish this objective **before** the workshop, and a number to the **right** to indicate how prepared you feel to accomplish the objective **after** attending this workshop.

1 Totally Unprepared	2	3 Moderately Prepared	4	5 Fully Prepared

BEFORE	Topic	AFTER
1 2 3 4 5	Using Adult Learning Principles	1 2 3 4 5
1 2 3 4 5	Analyzing the Training Requirement	1 2 3 4 5
1 2 3 4 5	Developing Learning Objectives	1 2 3 4 5
1 2 3 4 5	Outlining the Training Content	1 2 3 4 5
1 2 3 4 5	Developing a Training Plan	1 2 3 4 5
1 2 3 4 5	Using Facilitation Skills	1 2 3 4 5
1 2 3 4 5	Handling Problem Situations	1 2 3 4 5
1 2 3 4 5	Evaluating Training	1 2 3 4 5

PART 2

1. Did the workshop cover the training skills you need?   ❏ Yes   ❏ No

    If not, what else should have been included? _____

    _____

2. Do you think that the Coursebook materials are:

    a. Adequate for use during the workshop?   ❏ Yes   ❏ No

        If not, what changes would you suggest? _____

        _____

    b. Adequate for reference and use back on the job?   ❏ Yes   ❏ No

        If not, what changes would you suggest? _____

        _____

Lesson 13: Using the Training Skills

3. Was the time allotted:

   a. Appropriate for each of the lessons? ❏ Yes ❏ No

   If not, what changes would you suggest? _____

   _____

   b. Appropriate for the workshop as a whole? ❏ Yes ❏ No

   If not, what changes would you suggest? _____

   _____

4. Were appropriate training methods used? ❏ Yes ❏ No

   If not, what else should have been included? _____

   _____

5. Please rate the trainer's facilitation skills by circling the appropriate numbers on the chart.

		Low				High
a.	Attending	1	2	3	4	5
b.	Listening	1	2	3	4	5
c.	Questioning	1	2	3	4	5
d.	Responding	1	2	3	4	5

6. Which new skill will be most useful to you in your job? Why?

   _____

   _____

   _____

   _____

7. Any other comments?

   _____

   _____

   _____

   _____

Appendix: Job Aids

Purpose/Use

Now that you have completed ***Train-the-Trainer,*** you are ready to use your skills in developing and conducting training at work. The purpose of this Job Aids section is to help you do that. It contains:

Charts that summarize key ideas from lessons;

Worksheets for you to reproduce and use in completing training tasks;

Checklists to serve as memory-joggers along the way; and

References to help you find specific information in your Coursebook.

In preparing to develop and conduct your training, review the appropriate Coursebook sections first. Then use the job aids in this section as practical tools in completing the training tasks.

Use the chart below as a guide in completing all of the steps in the training process.

STEPS IN DEVELOPING AND CONDUCTING TRAINING	REVIEW COURSEBOOK SECTION	SEE JOB AID PAGES
Use adult learning principles	2	JA 2
Analyze the training requirement	3	JA 3–6
Develop learning objectives	4	JA 7–8
Outline the training content	5	JA 9-10
Select training methods	6	JA 11
Develop training aids	7	JA 12
Develop a lesson plan	8	JA 13–14
Conduct the training, using facilitation skills	9	JA 15
Evaluate the training	12	JA 16

Train-the-Trainer Participant Coursebook

Checklist: Adult Learning Principles

Use this checklist:

1. **Before** developing your training, in order to review and keep the principles in mind as you develop the training.

2. **During** the development of your training, in order to incorporate them into the training.

3. **After** you have developed your training, in order to verify that your training reflects these principles.

Does Your Training:

- ❏ Focus on "real world" problems?
- ❏ Emphasize how the learning can be applied?
- ❏ Relate the learning to the participant's goals?
- ❏ Relate the material to the participant's past experiences?
- ❏ Allow debate and challenge of ideas?
- ❏ Provide opportunities for you to listen to and respect the opinions of the participants?
- ❏ Encourage participants to be resources to you and to one another?
- ❏ Treat participants like adults?

References:

FOR MORE INFORMATION ABOUT...	SEE PAGE...
Differences between children and adults as participants	Coursebook 2-5

Worksheet: Analyzing the Training Requirement

Use the worksheet on the following pages as soon as you become aware of a training requirement in order to:

1. Organize the information you **have** about the potential training, and

2. Identify information you **need to obtain** in order to plan the training effectively.

References:

FOR MORE INFORMATION ABOUT . . .	SEE PAGE . . .
The worksheet elements	Coursebook 3-3
An example of a completed worksheet	Coursebook 3-7

Train-the-Trainer Participant Coursebook

Analyzing the Training Requirement: Worksheet

Today's date: _____

1. Statement of training need as requested:

2. Why is training required?

    a. Source of request:

    b. Expected benefits:

    c. Negative consequences if training is not delivered:

    d. New/changed behavior desired:

3. Who are the participants?

    a. Categories/size of participant groups:

    b. Familiarity with training content:

Analyzing the Training Requirement: Worksheet (continued)

4. What's the training content?

   a. Content:

   b. Available supporting resources
      (documentation, subject-matter experts, training packages):

   c. Issues/problems in formulating content:

   d. Anticipated reactions/problems with content/training:

5. What are the timing issues?

   a. Start data:

   b. Length of training:

   c. Frequency of training:

   d. Time issues:

Train-the-Trainer Participant Coursebook

Analyzing the Training Requirement: Worksheet (concluded)

6. Where will the training be conducted?

    a. Physical location:

    b. Estimated number of participants:

    c. Adequacy of space and delivery of resources needed:

Worksheet: Developing the Learning Objectives

Use the worksheet on the following page to identify the tasks participants should be able to perform as a result of training, and to develop learning objectives based on those tasks.

References:

For more information about . . .	See page . . .
Clarifying after-training tasks	Coursebook 4-3
Stating learning objectives	Coursebook 4-5

Train-the-Trainer Participant Coursebook

Developing the Learning Objectives

After-Training Tasks

Learning Objectives

Job Aids

Worksheet: Outlining the Training Content

Use the worksheet on the following pages to identify action steps and knowledge requirements, and to sequence the training content for one learning objective.

References:

FOR MORE INFORMATION ABOUT . . .	SEE PAGE . . .
Listing actions and knowledge requirements	Coursebook 5-3
Putting training content in sequence	Coursebook 5-4

Train-the-Trainer Participant Coursebook

Outlining the Training Content

Learning Objective

Actions and Knowledge Requirements

Information Summary: Training Methods

Use the following chart when selecting training methods for your lesson:

TRAINING METHOD	DESCRIPTION	ADVANTAGES	DISADVANTAGES
Case Study	Participants given hypothetical situation and asked to make a decision	Involves participants Stimulates "real world" thinking Can observe learning	Precision needed Can over-focus on content
Demonstration	Participants shown correct steps in completing a task	Aids in understanding Adds interest Provides model	Needs accuracy Preparation time
Group Discussion	Trainer leads group in discussing a topic	Involves participants Experiences are shared Can observe learning	Can be confusing Domination by one person possible
Role Play	Participants "act out" situations	Involves participants Can practice real situations	Can "over-act" Might be resistance to method
Structured Exercise	Participants take part in exercise using new skills	Aids in retention Involves participants	Preparation time Time consuming during training
Trainer Presentation	Trainer orally presents new information	Keeps group together Time control Can use with large group	Can be dull Limited retention

References:

FOR MORE INFORMATION ABOUT...	SEE PAGE...
General criteria for selecting methods	Coursebook 6-4

Information Summary: Training Aids

Use the following chart when selecting training aids to use in your lesson:

TRAINING AID	DESCRIPTION	ADVANTAGES	DISADVANTAGES
Video	Motion pictures with sound, recorded on cassette tape	Stimulate Motivate Illustrate	Costly Takes time Special equipment needed
Handouts	Written material prepared in advance and distributed during training	Can use later Individual pace Eliminate memorizing, note taking	Distracting Need updating
Flipcharts	Easel with blank pages to be written on with marker	Easily moved Reinforce learning Can use as outline	Must be neat Visibility problems
Slides	Information shown on an overhead projector	Professional Easily moved Can use with large group	Tiring glare Special equipment needed

References:

FOR MORE INFORMATION ABOUT...	SEE PAGE...
Steps for using video	Coursebook 7-4
Selecting and developing handouts	Coursebook 7-5, 7-6
Making flipcharts readable and appealing	Coursebook 7-7
Tips for using flipcharts	Coursebook 7-8
Making slides/transparencies readable and appealing	Coursebook 7-10
Guidelines for using slides/transparencies	Coursebook 7-11

Checklist: Developing a Lesson Plan

1. Use the two-column lesson plan format on the following page to develop your lesson plan.

2. Use the checklist below after you have developed your lesson plan and want to make sure that it is complete.

Does the Lesson Plan Include:

- ❑ Comments to introduce the topic to the participants?
- ❑ A way to have participants share what they know about the topic?
- ❑ An overview of the lesson, including the learning objective and why it is important?
- ❑ A **TELL** and **SHOW** for the training content being covered?
- ❑ An exercise?
- ❑ A summary that covers the main points?
- ❑ A transition statement to link to the next lesson or to the job?
- ❑ Specific questions at the appropriate points?
- ❑ References to training aids at the appropriate points?
- ❑ Allotted times for each segment?

References:

FOR MORE INFORMATION ABOUT...	SEE PAGE...
The ROPES model	Coursebook 8-2
Using the ROPES model	Coursebook 8-3
Allocating training time	Coursebook 8-5
The two-column lesson plan format	Coursebook 8-6
An example of a completed lesson plan	Coursebook 8-8

Lesson Plan Outline	Time/Training Aid

Checklist: Using Facilitation Skills in Training

Use this checklist:

1. **Before** you conduct your training, to remind yourself to use facilitation skills during the training.

2. **After** you conduct your training, to assess your use of facilitation skills during the training.

Did you . . .	Yes	No	N/A
1) Face the participants?	❏	❏	❏
2) Maintain eye contact?	❏	❏	❏
3) Move toward the participants?	❏	❏	❏
4) Avoid distractions?	❏	❏	❏
5) Demonstrate effective listening by paraphrasing?	❏	❏	❏
6) Ask effective questions?	❏	❏	❏
7) Appropriately handle participant responses to questions?	❏	❏	❏
8) Respond appropriately to participant questions?	❏	❏	❏

References:

FOR MORE INFORMATION ABOUT . . .	SEE PAGE . . .
Basic facilitation skills	Coursebook 9-2
Using attending skills	Coursebook 9-3
Observing participant behavior	Coursebook 9-4
Responding to inferences drawn about behaviors	Coursebook 9-5
Using listening skills	Coursebook 9-8
Asking questions	Coursebook 9-11
Handling participant responses to your questions	Coursebook 9-15
Responding to participant questions	Coursebook 9-16

Train-the-Trainer Participant Coursebook

Worksheet: Developing a Training Evaluation Plan

Use the worksheet below to consider the elements required for evaluating your training, and to chart the next steps you will take in planning for the evaluation.

References:

FOR MORE INFORMATION ABOUT . . .	SEE PAGE . . .
Levels of evaluation	Coursebook 12-4
Evaluation methods	Coursebook 12-7
Evaluation steps	Coursebook 12-8

Training Evaluation Plan Worksheet

Evaluation level(s) to be addressed:

❏ Reaction ❏ Learning ❏ Behaviors ❏ Results

Important data to gather:

_____
_____
_____

Data collection method(s) to be used:

❏ Questionnaire ❏ Interview
❏ Focus Group ❏ Observation
❏ Written Test ❏ Performance Records
❏ Performance Test

Next steps:

_____
_____
_____
_____
_____